**HBR'S
10
MUST
READS**

For
CEOs

HBR's 10 Must Reads series is the definitive collection of ideas and best practices for aspiring and experienced leaders alike. These books offer essential reading selected from the pages of *Harvard Business Review* on topics critical to the success of every manager.

Titles include:

HBR'S 10 MUST READS

For CEOs

HARVARD BUSINESS REVIEW PRESS

Boston, Massachusetts

The web addresses referenced in this book were live and correct at the time of the book's publication but may be subject to change.

Library of Congress Cataloging-in-Publication Data

Title: HBR's 10 must reads for CEOs.
Other titles: HBR's ten must reads for CEOs. | HBR's 10 must reads (Series)
Description: Boston, Massachusetts : Harvard Business Review Press, [2019] |
    Series: HBR's 10 must reads | Includes index.
Identifiers: LCCN 2018054311 | ISBN 978-1-63369-717-1
Subjects: LCSH: Chief executive officers. | Industrial management. |
    Strategic planning.
Classification: LCC HD38.2 .H394 2019 | DDC 658.4/2—dc23 LC record available
at https://lccn.loc.gov/2018054311

ISBN: 978-1-63369-717-1

Contents

Your Strategy Needs a Strategy

by Martin Reeves, Claire Love, and Philipp Tillmanns

THE OIL INDUSTRY HOLDS RELATIVELY few surprises for strategists. Things change, of course, sometimes dramatically, but in relatively predictable ways. Planners know, for instance, that global supply will rise and fall as geopolitical forces play out and new resources are discovered and exploited. They know that demand will rise and fall with incomes, GDPs, weather conditions, and the like. Because these factors are outside companies' and their competitors' control and barriers to entry are so high, no one is really in a position to change the game much. A company carefully marshals its unique capabilities and resources to stake out and defend its competitive position in this fairly stable firmament.

The internet software industry would be a nightmare for an oil industry strategist. Innovations and new companies pop up frequently, seemingly out of nowhere, and the pace at which companies can build—or lose—volume and market share is head-spinning. A major player like Microsoft or Google or Facebook can, without much warning, introduce some new platform or standard that fundamentally alters the basis of competition. In this environment, competitive advantage comes from reading and responding to signals faster than your rivals do, adapting quickly to change, or capitalizing on technological leadership to influence how demand and competition evolve.

When the Cold Winds Blow

THERE ARE CIRCUMSTANCES in which none of our strategic styles will work well: when access to capital or other critical resources is severely restricted, by either a sharp economic downturn or some other cataclysmic event. Such a harsh environment threatens the very viability of a company and demands a fifth strategic style—*survival*.

As its name implies, a survival strategy requires a company to focus defensively—reducing costs, preserving capital, trimming business portfolios. It is a short-term strategy, intended to clear the way for the company to live another day. But it does not lead to any long-term growth strategy. Companies in survival mode should therefore look ahead, readying themselves to assess the conditions of the new environment and to adopt an appropriate growth strategy once the crisis ends.

Clearly, the kinds of strategies that would work in the oil industry have practically no hope of working in the far less predictable and far less settled arena of internet software. And the skill sets that oil and software strategists need are worlds apart as well, because they operate on different time scales, use different tools, and have very different relationships with the people on the front lines who implement their plans. Companies operating in such dissimilar competitive environments should be planning, developing, and deploying their strategies in markedly different ways. But all too often, our research shows, they are not.

That is not for want of trying. Responses from a recent BCG survey of 120 companies around the world in 10 major industry sectors show that executives are well aware of the need to match their strategy-making processes to the specific demands of their competitive environments. Still, the survey found, in practice many rely instead on approaches that are better suited to predictable, stable environments, even when their own environments are known to be highly volatile or mutable.

What's stopping these executives from making strategy in a way that fits their situation? We believe they lack a systematic way to go about it—a strategy for making strategy. Here we present a simple framework that divides strategy planning into four styles according to how predictable your environment is and how much power

Idea in Brief

Companies that correctly match their strategy-making processes to their competitive circumstances perform better than those that don't. But too many use approaches appropriate only to predictable environments—even in highly volatile situations.

What executives in these cases need is a strategy for setting strategy. The authors present a framework for choosing one, which begins with two questions: How unpredictable is your environment? and How much power do you or others have to change that environment?

The answers give rise to four broad strategic styles, each one particularly suited to a distinct environment.

- **A classical strategy** (the one everyone learned in business school) works well for companies operating in predictable and immutable environments.

- **An adaptive strategy** is more flexible and experimental and works far better in immutable environments that are unpredictable.

- **A shaping strategy** is best in unpredictable environments that you have the power to change.

- **A visionary strategy** (the build-it-and-they-will-come approach) is appropriate in predictable environments that you have the power to change.

you have to change it. Using this framework, corporate leaders can match their strategic style to the particular conditions of their industry, business function, or geographic market.

How you set your strategy constrains the kind of strategy you develop. With a clear understanding of the strategic styles available and the conditions under which each is appropriate, more companies can do what we have found that the most successful are already doing—deploying their unique capabilities and resources to better capture the opportunities available to them.

Finding the Right Strategic Style

Strategy usually begins with an assessment of your industry. Your choice of strategic style should begin there as well. Although many industry factors will play into the strategy you actually formulate, you can narrow down your options by considering just two critical factors: *predictability* (How far into the future and how accurately can you confidently forecast demand, corporate performance, competitive dynamics, and market expectations?) and *malleability* (To what extent can you or your competitors influence those factors?).

Put these two variables into a matrix, and four broad strategic styles—which we label *classical, adaptive, shaping,* and *visionary*— emerge. (See the exhibit "The right strategic style for your environment.") Each style is associated with distinct planning practices and is best suited to one environment. Too often strategists conflate predictability and malleability—thinking that any environment that can be shaped is unpredictable—and thus divide the world of strategic possibilities into only two parts (predictable and immutable or unpredictable and mutable), whereas they ought to consider all four. So it did not surprise us to find that companies that match their strategic style to their environment perform significantly better than those that don't. In our analysis, the three-year total shareholder returns of companies in our survey that use the right style were 4% to 8% higher, on average, than the returns of those that do not.

Let's look at each style in turn.

Classical

When you operate in an industry whose environment is predictable but hard for your company to change, a classical strategic style has the best chance of success. This is the style familiar to most managers and business school graduates—five forces, blue ocean, and growth-share matrix analyses are all manifestations of it. A company sets a goal, targeting the most favorable market position it can attain by capitalizing on its particular capabilities and resources, and then tries to build and fortify that position through orderly, successive rounds of planning, using quantitative predictive methods that allow it to project well into the future. Once such plans are set, they tend to stay in place for several years. Classical strategic planning can work well as a stand-alone function because it requires special

The right strategic style for your environment

Our research shows that approaches to strategy formulation fall into four buckets, according to how predictable an industry's environment is and how easily companies can change that environment.

Adaptive
If your industry is unpredictable and you can't change it

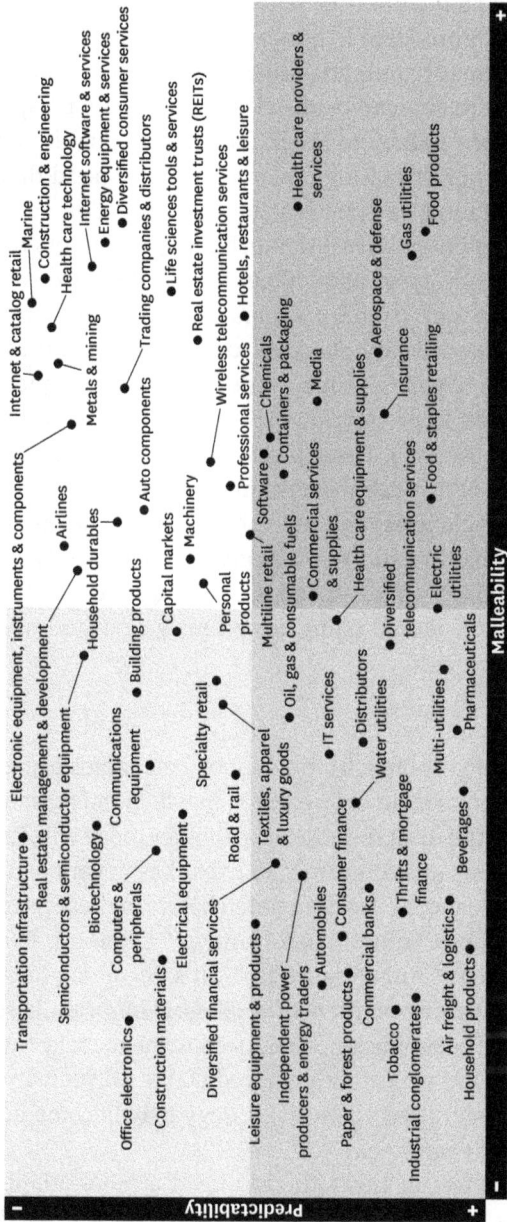

Shaping
If your industry is unpredictable but you can change it

Classical
If your industry is predictable but you can't change it

Visionary
If your industry is predictable and you can change it

Predictability (vertical axis, − to +)

Malleability (horizontal axis, − to +)

- Transportation infrastructure
- Real estate management & development
- Semiconductors & semiconductor equipment
- Biotechnology
- Computers & peripherals
- Office electronics
- Construction materials
- Electrical equipment
- Diversified financial services
- Leisure equipment & products
- Independent power producers & energy traders
- Automobiles
- Consumer finance
- Paper & forest products
- Commercial banks
- Tobacco
- Thrifts & mortgage finance
- Industrial conglomerates
- Air freight & logistics
- Household products
- Beverages
- Multi-utilities
- Pharmaceuticals
- Water utilities
- Distributors
- IT services
- Road & rail
- Textiles, apparel & luxury goods
- Specialty retail
- Oil, gas & consumable fuels
- Building products
- Communications equipment
- Household durables
- Airlines
- Electronic equipment, instruments & components
- Internet & catalog retail
- Marine
- Construction & engineering
- Health care technology
- Internet software & services
- Energy equipment & services
- Diversified consumer services
- Metals & mining
- Auto components
- Trading companies & distributors
- Life sciences tools & services
- Real estate investment trusts (REITs)
- Capital markets
- Machinery
- Personal products
- Wireless telecommunication services
- Professional services
- Hotels, restaurants & leisure
- Multiline retail
- Software
- Chemicals
- Containers & packaging
- Commercial services & supplies
- Media
- Health care equipment & supplies
- Diversified telecommunication services
- Insurance
- Aerospace & defense
- Electric utilities
- Food & staples retailing
- Gas utilities
- Food products
- Health care providers & services

Source: BCG analysis

analytic and quantitative skills, and things move slowly enough to allow for information to pass between departments.

Oil company strategists, like those in many other mature industries, effectively employ the classical style. At a major oil company such as ExxonMobil or Shell, for instance, highly trained analysts in the corporate strategic-planning office spend their days developing detailed perspectives on the long-term economic factors relating to demand and the technological factors relating to supply. These analyses allow them to devise upstream oil-extraction plans that may stretch 10 years into the future and downstream production-capacity plans up to five years out. It could hardly be otherwise, given the time needed to find and exploit new sources of oil, to build production facilities, and to keep them running at optimum capacity. These plans, in turn, inform multiyear financial forecasts, which determine annual targets that are focused on honing the efficiencies required to maintain and bolster the company's market position and performance. Only in the face of something extraordinary—an extended Gulf war; a series of major oil refinery shutdowns—would plans be seriously revisited more frequently than once a year.

Adaptive

The classical approach works for oil companies because their strategists operate in an environment in which the most attractive positions and the most rewarded capabilities today will, in all likelihood, remain the same tomorrow. But that has never been true for some industries, and, as has been noted before in these pages ("Adaptability: The New Competitive Advantage," by Martin Reeves and Mike Deimler, HBR July–August 2011), it's becoming less and less true where global competition, technological innovation, social feedback loops, and economic uncertainty combine to make the environment radically and persistently unpredictable. In such an environment, a carefully crafted classical strategy may become obsolete within months or even weeks.

Companies in this situation need a more adaptive approach, whereby they can constantly refine goals and tactics and shift, acquire, or divest resources smoothly and promptly. In such a fast-moving, reactive environment, when predictions are likely to be wrong and long-term plans are essentially useless, the goal cannot be to optimize efficiency; rather, it must be to engineer flexibility. Accordingly, planning cycles may shrink to less than a year or even become continual. Plans take the form not of carefully specified blueprints but of rough hypotheses based on the best available data. In testing them out, strategy must be tightly linked with or embedded in operations, to best capture change signals and minimize information loss and time lags.

Specialty fashion retailing is a good example of this. Tastes change quickly. Brands become hot (or not) overnight. No amount of data or planning will grant fashion executives the luxury of knowing far in advance what to make. So their best bet is to set up their organizations to continually produce, roll out, and test a variety of products as quickly as they can, constantly adapting production in the light of new learning.

The Spanish retailer Zara uses the adaptive approach. Zara does not rely heavily on a formal planning process; rather, its strategic style is baked into its flexible supply chain. It maintains strong ties with its 1,400 external suppliers, which work closely with its designers and marketers. As a result, Zara can design, manufacture, and ship a garment to its stores in as little as two to three weeks, rather than the industry average of four to six months. This allows the company to experiment with a wide variety of looks and make small bets with small batches of potentially popular styles. If they prove a hit, Zara can ramp up production quickly. If they don't, not much is lost in markdowns. (On average, Zara marks down only 15% of its inventory, whereas the figure for competitors can be as high as 50%.) So it need not predict or make bets on which fashions will capture its customers' imaginations and wallets from month to month. Instead it can respond quickly to information from its retail stores, constantly experiment with various offerings, and smoothly adjust to events as they play out.

Zara's strategic style requires relationships among its planners, designers, manufacturers, and distributors that are entirely different from what a company like ExxonMobil needs. Nevertheless, Exxon's strategists and Zara's designers have one critical thing in common: They take their competitive environment as a given and aim to carve out the best place they can within it.

Shaping

Some environments, as internet software vendors well know, can't be taken as given. For instance, in new or young high-growth industries where barriers to entry are low, innovation rates are high, demand is very hard to predict, and the relative positions of competitors are in flux, a company can often radically shift the course of industry development through some innovative move. A mature industry that's similarly fragmented and not dominated by a few powerful incumbents, or is stagnant and ripe for disruption, is also likely to be similarly malleable.

In such an environment, a company employing a classical or even an adaptive strategy to find the best possible market position runs the risk of selling itself short, being overrun by events, and missing opportunities to control its own fate. It would do better to employ a strategy in which the goal is to shape the unpredictable environment to its own advantage before someone else does—so that it benefits no matter how things play out.

Like an adaptive strategy, a shaping strategy embraces short or continual planning cycles. Flexibility is paramount, little reliance is placed on elaborate prediction mechanisms, and the strategy is most commonly implemented as a portfolio of experiments. But unlike adapters, shapers focus beyond the boundaries of their own company, often by rallying a formidable ecosystem of customers, suppliers, and/or complementors to their cause by defining attractive new markets, standards, technology platforms, and business practices. They propagate these through marketing, lobbying, and savvy partnerships. In the early stages of the digital revolution, internet software companies frequently used shaping strategies to create new communities, standards, and platforms that became the foundations for new markets and businesses.

That's essentially how Facebook overtook the incumbent MySpace in just a few years. One of Facebook's savviest strategic moves was to open its social-networking platform to outside developers in 2007, thus attracting all manner of applications to its site. Facebook couldn't hope to predict how big or successful any one of them would become. But it didn't need to. By 2008 it had attracted 33,000 applications; by 2010 that number had risen to more than 550,000. So as the industry developed and more than two-thirds of the successful social-networking apps turned out to be games, it was not surprising that the most popular ones—created by Zynga, Playdom, and Playfish—were operating from, and enriching, Facebook's site. What's more, even if the social-networking landscape shifts dramatically as time goes on, chances are the most popular applications will still be on Facebook. That's because by creating a flexible and popular platform, the company actively shaped the business environment to its own advantage rather than merely staking out a position in an existing market or reacting to changes, however quickly, after they'd occurred.

Visionary

Sometimes, not only does a company have the power to shape the future, but it's possible to know that future and to predict the path to realizing it. Those times call for bold strategies—the kind entrepreneurs use to create entirely new markets (as Edison did for electricity and Martine Rothblatt did for XM satellite radio), or corporate leaders use to revitalize a company with a wholly new vision—as Ratan Tata is trying to do with the ultra-affordable Nano automobile. These are the big bets, the build-it-and-they-will-come strategies.

Like a shaping strategist, the visionary considers the environment not as a given but as something that can be molded to advantage. Even so, the visionary style has more in common with a classical than with an adaptive approach. Because the goal is clear, strategists can take deliberate steps to reach it without having to keep many options open. It's more important for them to take the time and care they need to marshal resources, plan thoroughly, and implement correctly so that the vision doesn't fall victim to poor execution. Visionary strategists must have the courage to stay the course and the will to commit the necessary resources.

Back in 1994, for example, it became clear to UPS that the rise of internet commerce was going to be a bonanza for delivery companies, because the one thing online retailers would always need was a way to get their offerings out of cyberspace and onto their customers' doorsteps. This future may have been just as clear to the much younger and smaller FedEx, but UPS had the means—and the will—to make the necessary investments. That year it set up a cross-functional committee drawn from IT, sales, marketing, and finance to map out its path to becoming what the company later called "the enablers of global e-commerce." The committee identified the ambitious initiatives that UPS would need to realize this vision, which involved investing some $1 billion a year to integrate its core package-tracking operations with those of web providers and make acquisitions to expand its global delivery capacity. By 2000 UPS's multibillion-dollar bet had paid off: The company had snapped up a whopping 60% of the e-commerce delivery market.

Avoiding the Traps

In our survey, fully three out of four executives understood that they needed to employ different strategic styles in different circumstances. Yet judging by the practices they actually adopted, we estimate that the same percentage were using only the two strategic styles—classic and visionary—suited to predictable environments (see the exhibit "Which strategic style is used the most?"). That means only one in four was prepared in practice to adapt to unforeseeable events or to seize an opportunity to shape an industry to his or her company's advantage. Given our analysis of how unpredictable their business environments actually are, this number is far too low. Understanding how different the various approaches are and in which environment each best applies can go a long way toward correcting mismatches between strategic style and business environment. But as strategists think through the implications of the framework, they need to avoid three traps we have frequently observed.

Misplaced confidence
You can't choose the right strategic style unless you accurately judge how predictable and malleable your environment is. But when we

YOUR STRATEGY NEEDS A STRATEGY

Which strategic style is used the most?

Our survey found that companies were most often using the two styles best suited to predictable environments—classical and visionary—even when their environments were clearly unpredictable.

9%
Shaping

16%
Adaptive

35%
Classical

40%
Visionary

---

compared executives' perceptions with objective measures of their actual environments, we saw a strong tendency to overestimate both factors. Nearly half the executives believed they could control uncertainty in the business environment through their own actions. More than 80% said that achieving goals depended on their own actions more than on things they could not control.

Unexamined habits

Many executives recognized the importance of building the adaptive capabilities required to address unpredictable environments, but fewer than one in five felt sufficiently competent in them. In part that's because many executives learned only the classical style, through experience or at business school. Accordingly, we weren't surprised to find that nearly 80% said that in practice they begin their strategic planning by articulating a goal and then analyzing how best to get there. What's more, some 70% said that in practice they value accuracy over speed of decisions, even when they are well aware that their environment is fast-moving and unpredictable. As a result, a lot of time is being wasted making untenable predictions

Are You Clinging to the Wrong Strategy Style?

A **CLEAR ESTIMATION** of your industry's predictability and malleability is key to picking the right strategy style. But our survey of more than 120 companies in 10 industries showed that companies don't do this well: Their estimates rarely matched our objective measures. They consistently *overestimated* both predictability and malleability.

when a faster, more iterative, and more experimental approach would be more effective. Executives are also closely attuned to quarterly and annual financial reporting, which heavily influences their strategic-planning cycles. Nearly 90% said they develop strategic plans on an annual basis, regardless of the actual pace of change in their business environments—or even what they perceive it to be.

Culture mismatches

Although many executives recognize the importance of adaptive capabilities, it can be highly countercultural to implement them. Classical strategies aimed at achieving economies of scale and scope often create company cultures that prize efficiency and the elimination of variation. These can of course undermine the opportunity to experiment and learn, which is essential for an adaptive strategy. And failure is a natural outcome of experimentation, so adaptive and shaping strategies fare poorly in cultures that punish it.

Avoiding some of these traps can be straightforward once the differing requirements of the four strategic styles are understood. Simply being aware that adaptive planning horizons don't necessarily correlate well with the rhythms of financial markets, for instance, might go a long way toward eliminating ingrained planning habits. Similarly, understanding that the point of shaping and visionary strategies is to change the game rather than to optimize your position in the market may be all that's needed to avoid starting with the wrong approach.

Being more thoughtful about metrics is also helpful. Although companies put a great deal of energy into making predictions year after year, it's surprising how rarely they check to see if the predictions they made in the prior year actually panned out. We suggest regularly reviewing the accuracy of your forecasts and also objectively gauging predictability by tracking how often and to what extent companies in your industry change relative position in terms of revenue, profitability, and other performance measures. To get a better sense of the extent to which industry players can change their environment, we recommend measuring industry youthfulness, concentration, growth rate, innovation rate, and rate of technology change—all of which increase malleability.

Operating in Many Modes

Matching your company's strategic style to the predictability and malleability of your industry will align overall strategy with the broad economic conditions in which the company operates. But various company units may well operate in differing subsidiary or geographic markets that are more or less predictable and malleable than the industry at large. Strategists in these units and markets can use the same process to select the most effective style for their particular circumstances, asking themselves the same initial questions: How predictable is the environment in which our unit operates? How much power do we have to change that environment? The answers may vary widely. We estimate, for example, that the Chinese business environment overall has been almost twice as malleable and unpredictable as that in the United States, making shaping strategies often more appropriate in China.

Similarly, the functions within your company are likely to operate in environments that call for differing approaches to departmental planning. It's easy to imagine, for instance, that within the auto industry a classical style would work well for optimizing production but would be inappropriate for the digital marketing department, which probably has a far greater power to shape its environment (after all, that's what advertising aims to do) and would hardly benefit from mapping out its campaigns years in advance.

The Ultimate in Strategic Flexibility

HAIER, A CHINESE HOME-APPLIANCE MANUFACTURER, may have taken strategic flexibility just about as far as it can go. The company has devised a system in which units as small as an individual can effectively use differing styles.

How does it manage this? Haier's organization comprises thousands of minicompanies, each accountable for its own P&L. Any employee can start one of them. But there are no cost centers in the company—only profit centers. Each minicompany bears the fully loaded costs of its operations, and each party negotiates with the others for services; even the finance department sells its services to the others. Every employee is held accountable for achieving profits. An employee's salary is based on a simple formula: base salary × % of monthly target achieved + bonus (or deduction) based on individual P&L. In other words, if a minicompany achieves none of its monthly target (0%), the employees in it receive no salary that month.

Operating at this level of flexibility can be as rewarding as it is daunting. Near bankruptcy in 1985, Haier has since become the world's largest home-appliance company—ahead of LG, Samsung, GE, and Whirlpool.

If units or functions within your company would benefit from operating in a strategic style other than the one best suited to your industry as a whole, it follows that you will very likely need to manage more than one strategic style at a time. Executives in our survey are well aware of this: In fact, fully 90% aspired to improve their ability to manage multiple styles simultaneously. The simplest but also the least flexible way to do this is to structure and run functions, regions, or business units that require differing strategic styles separately. Allowing teams within units to select their own styles gives you more flexibility in diverse or fast-changing environments but is generally more challenging to realize. (For an example of a company that has found a systematic way to do it, see the sidebar "The Ultimate in Strategic Flexibility.")

Finally, a company moving into a different stage of its life cycle may well require a shift in strategic style. Environments for start-ups tend to be malleable, calling for visionary or shaping strategies. In a company's growth and maturity phases, when the environment is less malleable, adaptive or classical styles are often best. For companies in a declining phase, the environment becomes more malleable again, generating opportunities for disruption and rejuvenation through either a shaping or a visionary strategy.

Once you have correctly analyzed your environment, not only for the business as a whole but for each of your functions, divisions, and geographic markets, and you have identified which strategic styles should be used, corrected for your own biases, and taken steps to prime your company's culture so that the appropriate styles can successfully be applied, you will need to monitor your environment and be prepared to adjust as conditions change over time. Clearly that's no easy task. But we believe that companies that continually match their strategic styles to their situation will enjoy a tremendous advantage over those that don't.

Originally published in September 2012. Reprint R1209E

Managing Your Innovation Portfolio

by Bansi Nagji and Geoff Tuff

MANAGEMENT KNOWS IT and so does Wall Street: The year-to-year viability of a company depends on its ability to innovate. Given today's market expectations, global competitive pressures, and the extent and pace of structural change, this is truer than ever. But chief executives struggle to make the case to the Street that their managerial actions can be relied on to yield a stream of successful new offerings. Many admit to being unsure and frustrated. Typically they are aware of a tremendous amount of innovation going on inside their enterprises but don't feel they have a grasp on all the dispersed initiatives. The pursuit of the new feels haphazard and episodic, and they suspect that the returns on the company's total innovation investment are too low.

Making matters worse, executives tend to respond with dramatic interventions and vacillating strategies. Take the example of a consumer goods company we know. Attuned to the need to keep its brands fresh in retailers' and consumers' minds, it introduced frequent improvements and variations on its core offerings. Most of those earned their keep with respectable uptake by the market and decent margins. Over time, however, it became clear that all this product proliferation, while splitting the revenue pie into ever-smaller slices, wasn't actually growing the pie. Eager to achieve a much higher return, management lurched toward a new strategy aimed at breakthrough product development—at transformational rather than incremental innovations.

Unfortunately, this company's structure and processes were not set up to execute on that ambition; although it had the requisite capabilities for envisioning, developing, and market testing innovations close to its core, it neither recognized nor gained the very different capabilities needed to take a bolder path. Its most inventive ideas ended up being diluted beyond recognition, killed outright, or crushed under the weight of the enterprise. Before long the company retreated to what it knew best. Once again, little was ventured and little was gained—and the cycle repeated itself.

We tell this story because it is typical of companies that have not yet learned to manage innovation strategically. It demonstrates an all-too-common contrast to the steady, above-average returns that can be achieved only through a well-balanced portfolio. The companies we've found to have the strongest innovation track records can articulate a clear innovation ambition; have struck the right balance of core, adjacent, and transformational initiatives across the enterprise; and have put in place the tools and capabilities to manage those various initiatives as parts of an integrated whole. Rather than hoping that their future will emerge from a collection of ad hoc, stand-alone efforts that compete with one another for time, money, attention, and prestige, they manage for "total innovation."

Be Clear About Your Innovation Ambition

What does it mean to manage an innovation portfolio? First, let's consider how broad a term "innovation" is. Defined as a novel creation that produces value, an innovation can be as slight as a new nail polish color or as vast as the World Wide Web. Most companies invest in initiatives along a broad spectrum of risk and reward. As in financial investing, their goal should be to construct the portfolio that produces the highest overall return that's in keeping with their appetite for risk.

One tool we've developed is the Innovation Ambition Matrix (see the exhibit "The Innovation Ambition Matrix"). Students of management will recognize it as a refinement of a classic diagram

Idea in Brief

Firms pursue innovation at three levels of ambition: enhancements to core offerings, pursuit of adjacent opportunities, and ventures into transformational territory.

Analysis of innovation investments and returns reveals two striking findings. Firms that outperform their peers tend to allocate their investments in a certain ratio: 70% to safe bets in the core, 20% to less sure things in adjacent spaces, and 10% to high-risk transformational initiatives. As it happens, an inverse ratio applies to returns on innovation.

Although never the dominant activity, transformational initiatives are vital to a company's ongoing health, and firms must recognize that they demand unique management approaches.

- Talent should include a diverse set of skills and be able to deal with ambiguous data.

- Teams should be separated from day-to-day operations.

- Funding should come from outside the normal budget cycle.

- Pipeline management should focus on the iterative development of a few promising ideas, not the ruthless filtering of many.

- Metrics should recognize non-financial achievements in early phases.

devised by the mathematician H. Igor Ansoff to help companies allocate funds among growth initiatives. Ansoff's matrix clarified the notion that tactics should differ according to whether a firm was launching a new product, entering a new market, or both. Our version replaces Ansoff's binary choices of product and market (old versus new) with a range of values. This acknowledges that the novelty of a company's offerings (on the x axis) and the novelty of its customer markets (on the y axis) are a matter of degree. We have overlaid three levels of distance from the company's current, bottom-left reality.

In the band of activity at the lower left of the matrix are core innovation initiatives—efforts to make incremental changes to existing products and incremental inroads into new markets. Whether in the form of new packaging (such as Nabisco's 100-calorie packets of Oreos for on-the-go snackers), slight reformulations (as when Dow Agro-Sciences launched one of its herbicides as a liquid suspension rather than a dry powder), or added service convenience (for example,

The Innovation Ambition Matrix

Firms that excel at total innovation management simultaneously invest at three levels of ambition, carefully managing the balance among them.

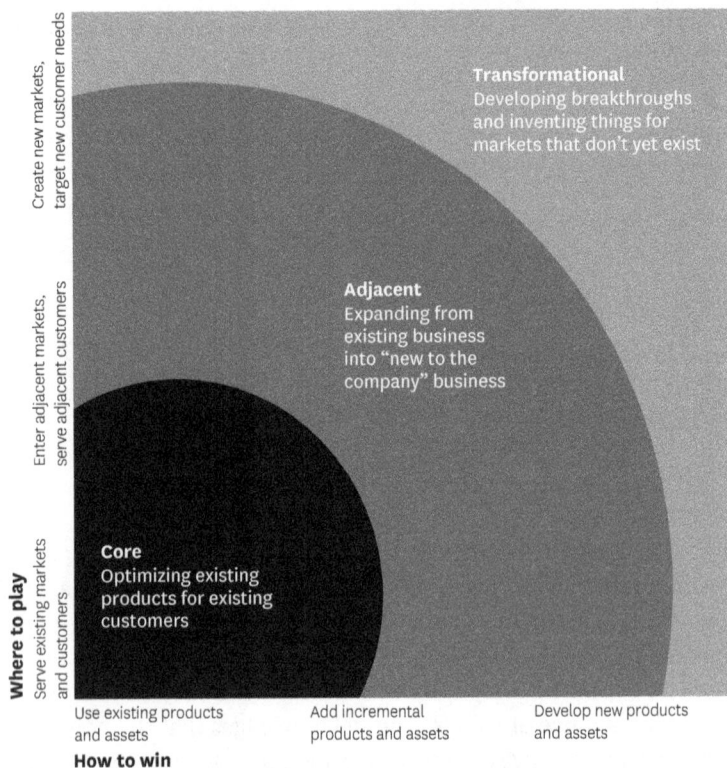

Where to play

Create new markets, target new customer needs

Enter adjacent markets, serve adjacent customers

Serve existing markets and customers

Transformational
Developing breakthroughs and inventing things for markets that don't yet exist

Adjacent
Expanding from existing business into "new to the company" business

Core
Optimizing existing products for existing customers

Use existing products and assets

Add incremental products and assets

Develop new products and assets

How to win

replacing pallets with shrink-wrapping to reduce shipping charges), such innovations draw on assets the company already has in place.

At the opposite corner of the matrix are transformational initiatives, designed to create new offers—if not whole new businesses—to serve new markets and customer needs. These are the innovations that, when successful, make headlines: Think of iTunes, the Tata Nano, and the Starbucks in-store experience. These sorts of innovations, also called breakthrough, disruptive, or game changing, generally require that the company call on unfamiliar assets—for example, building capabilities to gain a deeper understanding of customers, to communicate about products that have no direct antecedents, and to develop markets that aren't yet mature.

In the middle are adjacent innovations, which can share characteristics with core and transformational innovations. An adjacent innovation involves leveraging something the company does well into a new space. Procter & Gamble's Swiffer is a case in point. It arose from a set of needs P&G knew well and built on customers' assumption that the proper tool for cleaning floors is a long-handled mop. But it used a novel technology to take the solution to a new customer set and generate new revenue streams. Adjacent innovations allow a company to draw on existing capabilities but necessitate putting those capabilities to new uses. They require fresh, proprietary insight into customer needs, demand trends, market structure, competitive dynamics, technology trends, and other market variables.

The Innovation Ambition Matrix offers no inherent prescription. Its power lies in the two exercises it facilitates. First, it gives managers a framework for surveying all the initiatives the business has under way: How many are being pursued in each realm, and how much investment is going to each type of innovation? Second, it gives managers a way to discuss the right *overall* ambition for the company's innovation portfolio. For one company—say, a consumer goods producer—succeeding as a great innovator might mean investing in initiatives that tend toward the lower left, such as small extensions to existing product lines. A high-tech company might move toward the upper right, taking bigger risks on more-audacious innovations for the chance of bigger payoffs. Although this may sound obvious, few organizations think about the best level of innovation to target, and fewer still manage to achieve it.

Strike and Maintain the Right Balance

In contemplating the balance for an innovation portfolio, managers should consider the findings of research we conducted recently. In a study of companies in the industrial, technology, and consumer goods sectors, we looked at whether any particular allocation of resources across core, adjacent, and transformational initiatives correlated with significantly better performance as reflected in share price. Indeed, the data revealed a pattern: Companies that allocated about 70% of their innovation activity to core initiatives, 20% to adjacent ones, and 10% to transformational ones outperformed their peers, typically realizing a P/E premium of 10% to 20% (see the exhibit "Is there a golden ratio?"). Google knows this well: Cofounder Larry Page told *Fortune* magazine that the company strives for a 70-20-10 balance, and he credited the 10% of resources that are dedicated to transformational efforts with all the company's truly new offerings. Our subsequent conversations with buy-side analysts revealed that this allocation is attractive to capital markets because of what it implies about the balance between short-term, predictable growth and longer-term bets.

A second research finding adds more food for thought. In an ongoing study, we're focusing on more-direct returns on innovation.

Is there a golden ratio?

Analysis reveals that the allocation of resources shown below correlates with meaningfully higher share price performance. For most companies, this breakdown is a good starting point for discussion.

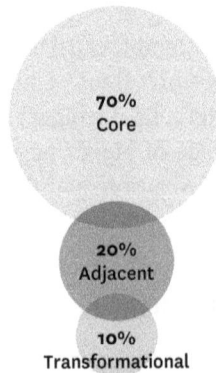

70%
Core

20%
Adjacent

10%
Transformational

Of the bottom-line gains companies enjoy as a result of their innovation efforts, what proportions are generated by core, adjacent, and transformational initiatives? We're finding consistently that the return ratio is roughly the inverse of that ideal allocation described above: Core innovation efforts typically contribute 10% of the long-term, cumulative return on innovation investment; adjacent initiatives contribute 20%; and transformational efforts contribute 70% (see the exhibit "How innovation pays the bills").

Together these findings underscore the importance of managing total innovation deliberately and closely. Most companies are heavily oriented toward core innovation—and must continue to be, given the risk involved in adjacent and transformational initiatives. But if that natural tendency leads to neglect of more-ambitious forms of innovation, the outcome will be a steady decline in business and relevance to customers. Transformational initiatives are the engines of blockbuster growth.

How innovation pays the bills

Among high performers that invest in all three levels of innovation, we find the following distribution of total returns. As it happens, this ratio is the inverse of the resource allocation ratio we discovered in high-performing companies.

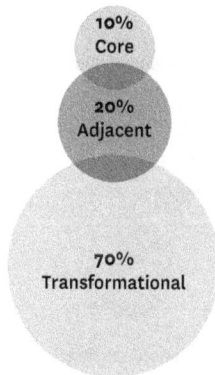

10%
Core

20%
Adjacent

70%
Transformational

Let us be clear: We're not suggesting that a 70-20-10 breakdown of innovation investment is a magic formula for all companies; it's simply an average allocation based on a cross-industry and cross-geography analysis. The right balance will vary from company to company according to a number of factors (see the exhibit "Different ambitions, different allocations").

One important factor is industry. The industrial manufacturers we studied have a strong portfolio of core innovations complemented by a few breakouts, and they come closest to the 70-20-10 breakdown. Technology companies spend less time and money on improving core products, because their market is eager for the next hot release. Consumer packaged goods manufacturers have little activity at the transformational level, because their main focus is incremental innovation. Of these three sorts of businesses, industrial manufacturers collectively have the highest P/E ratio relative to their peers, perhaps suggesting that they are closest to getting the balance right—for them.

Different ambitions, different allocations

On average, high-performing firms direct 70% of their innovation resources to enhancements of core offerings, 20% to adjacent opportunities, and 10% to transformational initiatives. But individual firms may deviate from that ratio for sound strategic reasons. Here are three allocations we have seen that made sense for firms in various circumstances.

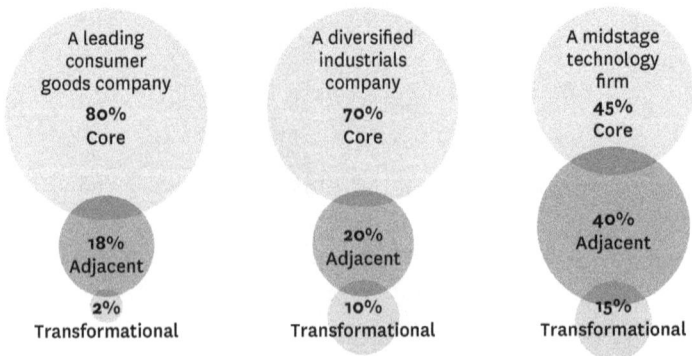

A leading consumer goods company
80% Core
18% Adjacent
2% Transformational

A diversified industrials company
70% Core
20% Adjacent
10% Transformational

A midstage technology firm
45% Core
40% Adjacent
15% Transformational

A company's competitive position within its industry also influences the balance. For example, a lagging company might want to pursue more high-risk transformational innovation in the hope of creating a truly disruptive product or service that would dramatically alter its growth curve. A struggling Apple made this decision in the late 1990s, effectively betting its business on several bold initiatives, including the iTunes platform. A company that wants to retain its leadership position or believes the market for its more ambitious innovations has cooled may decide to do the reverse, removing some risk from its portfolio by shifting its emphasis from transformational to core initiatives.

A third factor is a company's stage of development. Early-stage enterprises, especially those funded by venture capital, must make a big splash. They may feel that a disproportionate investment in transformational innovation is warranted, both to attract media attention, investors, and customers, and because they don't yet have much of a core business to build on. As they mature and develop a stable customer base, and as protecting and growing the core becomes more important, they may shift their emphasis toward that of a more established company.

The point is that a management team should arrive at a ratio that it believes will deliver better ROI in the form of revenue growth and market capitalization, should discover how far its current allocation is from that ideal, and should come up with a plan to close the gap.

Organize and Manage the Total Innovation System

Targeting a healthy balance of core, adjacent, and transformational innovation is a vital step toward managing a total innovation portfolio, but it immediately raises an issue: To realize the promise of that balance, a company must be able to execute at all three levels of ambition. Unfortunately, the managerial toolbox required to keep innovation on track varies greatly according to the type of innovation in question. Few companies are good at all three.

Companies typically struggle the most with transformational innovation. A study by the Corporate Strategy Board shows that mature companies attempting to enter new businesses fail as often as 99% of the time. This reflects the hard truth that to achieve transformation—to do different things—an organization usually has to *do things differently*. It needs different people, different motivational factors, and different support systems. The ones that get it right (GE and IBM are notable examples) have thought carefully about five key areas of management that serve the three levels of innovation ambition.

Talent

The skills needed for core and adjacent innovations are quite different from those needed for transformational innovations. In the first two realms, analytical skills are vital, because such initiatives call for market and customer data to be interpreted and translated into specific offering enhancements. Procter & Gamble, for example, deploys a cadre of 70 senior employees around the world to help identify promising adjacencies. These "technology entrepreneurs," as the company calls them, are responsible for researching a variety of sources, including scientific journals and patent databases, and for physically observing activities in specific markets in order to find new ideas that can build on P&G's core businesses. The company credits its technology entrepreneurs with uncovering more than 10,000 potential offerings for review.

Transformational innovation efforts, by contrast, typically employ a discovery and concept-development process to uncover and analyze the social needs driving business changes (what's desirable from a customer perspective), the underlying market trends (what kinds of offers might be viable), and ongoing technological developments (what is feasible to produce and sell). These activities require skills found among designers, cultural anthropologists, scenario planners, and analysts who are comfortable with ambiguous data. Thus, when Samsung decided to compete on the basis of innovative design, it recognized that it needed new and different skills. The company moved its design center from a small town to Seoul in order to be closer to a valuable pool of young design professionals. It also teamed with a number of outside firms with strong design skills and created an in-house school, led by industrial design experts, to hone the abilities of designers who exhibited potential. The results speak for themselves: In a decade Samsung has garnered numerous design awards while evolving from a manufacturer of nondescript consumer electronics to one of the most valuable brands in the world.

Integration

Although the right skills are critical, they are not sufficient. They must be organized and managed in the right way, with the right mandate, and under the conditions that will help them succeed. One of the most important decisions will be how closely to connect the skills and associated activities with the day-to-day business.

In most companies, the majority of people engaged in innovation are working on enhancements to core offerings; they're most likely to succeed if they remain integrated with the existing business. Even teams working on adjacent innovations benefit from the efficiencies that come with close ties to the core business, assuming they're given the appropriate tools to take their work further afield.

However, as Samsung's move suggests, transformational innovation tends to benefit when the people involved are separated from the core business—financially, organizationally, and sometimes physically. Without that distance, they can't escape the gravitational pull of the company's norms and expectations, all of which reinforce an emphasis on sustaining the core.

Funding

Most efforts related to core and adjacent innovation are fairly small-scale projects that don't need major infusions of cash. They can and should be funded by the relevant business unit's P&L through annual budget cycles.

Bold transformational efforts typically require sustained—and sometimes significant—investment. Their funding should come from an entity (perhaps the executive suite, and ideally the CEO) that can rise above the fray of annual budget allocation. But companies should avoid the "innovation tax" approach, whereby the

C-suite asks all areas of the business to contribute a percentage of their budgets to transformational initiatives (under the theory that innovation benefits the whole company, so everyone should support it). Business units rarely see their "contribution" as going to a good cause; they simply perceive that the corporate office is siphoning off 5% of their budgets, and come to regard the innovation team as the bad guys.

Companies might instead create a completely different funding structure for transformational innovation, one that's separate from the regular P&Ls of the business. An example is Merck's Global Health Innovation venture fund, a separate limited liability corporation that invests in interesting health care companies operating at the periphery of Merck's core pharmaceutical, vaccines, and consumer health businesses. The main purpose of the fund is to place bets on components of an evolved future business model for the company. It is also used on occasion to fund organic innovation initiatives, such as Merck Breakthrough Open, a crowdsourcing forum that solicits employee ideas for transformational growth opportunities.

Pipeline management

Any well-managed innovation process includes mechanisms to track ongoing initiatives and ensure that they are progressing according to plan. Companies typically rely on stage-gate processes to assess projects periodically, recalculate their projected ROI according to any changed conditions, and decide whether they should get a green light. But such projections are only as reliable as the market insight the company can glean. In the case of a core product extension, that insight is usually sufficient: Customers can say whether they would like a proposed product variant and, if so, how much they'd be willing to pay for it. However, if the innovation initiative involves an entirely new solution—one that customers may not even know they need—traditional stage-gate processes are dangerous. It's impossible to predict fifth-year sales for something the world has never seen before.

Moreover, whereas pipeline management for core or near-adjacent innovation involves gradually finding a small set of winners from among a vast number of ideas, the process is very different for transformational innovation. Here the challenge is to take a small number of possibly game-changing ideas and ensure that they emerge from the pipeline stronger. A company must spend sufficient time up front exploring what's possible, constantly expanding the options available in pursuit of the right big idea. In other words, transformational efforts are not generally managed with a funnel approach; they require a nonlinear process in which potential alternatives remain undefined for a long period of time. This is another reason why a stage-gate process is so lethal to transformational innovation: It results in the rejection of promising options before they are properly explored.

Metrics

Finally, there is the question of what measurements should inform management. For core or adjacent initiatives, traditional financial metrics are entirely appropriate. But using such metrics too early in transformational efforts can kill potentially great ideas. For instance, net present value and ROI calculations, commonly used to assess core and near-adjacent initiatives, require assumptions about adoption rates, price points, and other key variables—which in turn require customer input. Such input is impossible to obtain for something the world does not yet know it needs.

Managers should discuss thoughtfully where economic and non-economic metrics, along with external and internal metrics, are most appropriate. Stage-gate systems operate at the intersection of *economic* and *external* metrics—they estimate how much money the company will make when its innovation is launched in the outside world. And, again, this combination is appropriate for evaluating core or near-adjacent initiatives on the basis of information that is obtainable and largely accurate.

Companies should use the polar opposite—a combination of *non-economic* and *internal* metrics—to assess transformational efforts in their early stages; this can enhance the team's ability to learn and explore. For example, what if the only hurdle an initiative must clear to receive continued investment is that the company is likely to *learn* (not earn) from it? That is how Google has assessed transformational innovation from the start.

Eventually a company must focus on the hard economics of a transformational project. But that can wait until there's something ready to pilot and launch.

Moving Forward

Managing total innovation will require a significant shift for most companies, which are used to a less orderly approach. But the pathway to such discipline is clear. The first step is to develop a shared sense of the role innovation plays in driving the organization's growth and competitiveness. Managers should agree on an appropriate ambition level for innovation and find common language to describe it.

Next, it makes sense to survey the company's current innovation landscape. A comprehensive audit will reveal how much time, effort, and money are allocated to core, adjacent, and transformational initiatives—and how that allocation differs from the ideal ratio for the company in question. With the difference exposed, managers can identify ways to achieve the desired balance, usually by paring core initiatives down to those focused on the highest-value customers, encouraging more initiatives in the adjacent space, and creating conditions more conducive to breakthroughs in the transformational realm.

Throughout all this activity, leaders must communicate clearly and relentlessly about innovation goals and processes. There's no getting around the fact that to improve the overall return on innovation investments, managers must take a hard look at projects—all of which are attached to people who feel a sense of ownership and pride in them. The imperative is to identify and accelerate the most promising ideas and kill off the rest (some of which may be perfectly viable but don't represent the best use of resources). Open commitments and clear messaging will go a long way toward ensuring that the entire organization knows what is being decided by whom and why, and how those decisions will benefit the business over the short and long terms.

For many companies, innovation will remain a sprawling collection of activities, energetic but uncoordinated. And for many managers, it will remain a source of frustration. For the best managers, however, it represents the most exciting and important challenge of all. By figuring out how to manage innovation as an integrated system within overall portfolio goals, they can harness its energy and make it a reliable driver of growth.

Originally published in May 2012. Reprint R1205C

Leading Change

Why Transformation Efforts Fail. *by John P. Kotter*

Editor's Note: Guiding change may be the ultimate test of a leader—no business survives over the long term if it can't reinvent itself. But, human nature being what it is, fundamental change is often resisted mightily by the people it most affects: those in the trenches of the business. Thus, leading change is both absolutely essential and incredibly difficult.

Perhaps nobody understands the anatomy of organizational change better than retired Harvard Business School professor John P. Kotter. This article, originally published in the spring of 1995, previewed Kotter's 1996 book Leading Change. *It outlines eight critical success factors—from establishing a sense of extraordinary urgency, to creating short-term wins, to changing the culture ("the way we do things around here"). It will feel familiar when you read it, in part because Kotter's vocabulary has entered the lexicon and in part because it contains the kind of home truths that we recognize, immediately, as if we'd always known them. Two decades later, his work on leading change remains definitive.*

OVER THE PAST DECADE, I have watched more than 100 companies try to remake themselves into significantly better competitors. They have included large organizations (Ford) and small ones (Landmark Communications), companies based in the United States (General Motors) and elsewhere (British Airways), corporations that were on their knees (Eastern Airlines), and companies that were earning good money (Bristol-Myers Squibb). These efforts have gone under many banners: total quality management, reengineering,

Eight steps to transforming your organization

1 **Establishing a sense of urgency**
- Examining market and competitive realities
- Identifying and discussing crises, potential crises, or major opportunities

2 **Forming a powerful guiding coalition**
- Assembling a group with enough power to lead the change effort
- Encouraging the group to work together as a team

3 **Creating a vision**
- Creating a vision to help direct the change effort
- Developing strategies for achieving that vision

4 **Communicating the vision**
- Using every vehicle possible to communicate the new vision and strategies
- Teaching new behaviors by the example of the guiding coalition

5 **Empowering others to act on the vision**
- Getting rid of obstacles to change
- Changing systems or structures that seriously undermine the vision
- Encouraging risk taking and nontraditional ideas, activities, and actions

6 **Planning for and creating short-term wins**
- Planning for visible performance improvements
- Creating those improvements
- Recognizing and rewarding employees involved in the improvements

7 **Consolidating improvements and producing still more change**
- Using increased credibility to change systems, structures, and policies that don't fit the vision
- Hiring, promoting, and developing employees who can implement the vision
- Reinvigorating the process with new projects, themes, and change agents

8 **Institutionalizing new approaches**
- Articulating the connections between the new behaviors and corporate success
- Developing the means to ensure leadership development and succession

Idea in Brief

Most major change initiatives—whether intended to boost quality, improve culture, or reverse a corporate death spiral—generate only lukewarm results. Many fail miserably.

Why? Kotter maintains that too many leaders don't realize transformation is a *process*, not an event. It advances through stages that build on each other. And it takes years. Pressured to accelerate the process, leaders skip stages. But shortcuts never work.

Equally troubling, even highly capable leaders make critical mistakes—such as declaring victory too soon. Result? Loss of momentum, reversal of hard-won gains, and devastation of the entire transformation effort.

By understanding the stages of change—and the pitfalls unique to each stage—you boost your chances of a successful transformation. The payoff? Your organization flexes with tectonic shifts in competitors, markets, and technologies—leaving rivals far behind.

rightsizing, restructuring, cultural change, and turnaround. But, in almost every case, the basic goal has been the same: to make fundamental changes in how business is conducted in order to help cope with a new, more challenging market environment.

A few of these corporate change efforts have been very successful. A few have been utter failures. Most fall somewhere in between, with a distinct tilt toward the lower end of the scale. The lessons that can be drawn are interesting and will probably be relevant to even more organizations in the increasingly competitive business environment of the coming decade.

The most general lesson to be learned from the more successful cases is that the change process goes through a series of phases that, in total, usually require a considerable length of time. Skipping steps creates only the illusion of speed and never produces a satisfying result. A second very general lesson is that critical mistakes in any of the phases can have a devastating impact, slowing momentum and negating hard-won gains. Perhaps because we have relatively little experience in renewing organizations, even very capable people often make at least one big error.

Idea in Practice

To give your transformation effort the best chance of succeeding, take the right actions at each stage—and avoid common pitfalls.

Stage	Actions needed	Pitfalls
Establish a sense of urgency	• Examine market and competitive realities for potential crises and untapped opportunities. • Convince at least 75% of your managers that the status quo is more dangerous than the unknown.	• Underestimating the difficulty of driving people from their comfort zones • Becoming paralyzed by risks
Form a powerful guiding coalition	• Assemble a group with shared commitment and enough power to lead the change effort. • Encourage them to work as a team outside the normal hierarchy.	• No prior experience in teamwork at the top • Relegating team leadership to an HR, quality, or strategic-planning executive rather than a senior line manager
Create a vision	• Create a vision to direct the change effort. • Develop strategies for realizing that vision.	• Presenting a vision that's too complicated or vague to be communicated in five minutes
Communicate the vision	• Use every vehicle possible to communicate the new vision and strategies for achieving it. • Teach new behaviors by the example of the guiding coalition.	• Undercommunicating the vision • Behaving in ways antithetical to the vision

Error 1: Not Establishing a Great Enough Sense of Urgency

Most successful change efforts begin when some individuals or some groups start to look hard at a company's competitive situation, market position, technological trends, and financial

Empower others to act on the vision	• Remove or alter systems or structures undermining the vision. • Encourage risk taking and nontraditional ideas, activities, and actions.	• Failing to remove powerful individuals who resist the change effort
Plan for and create short-term wins	• Define and engineer visible performance improvements. • Recognize and reward employees contributing to those improvements.	• Leaving short-term successes up to chance • Failing to score successes early enough (12–24 months into the change effort)
Consolidate improvements and produce more change	• Use increased credibility from early wins to change systems, structures, and policies undermining the vision. • Hire, promote, and develop employees who can implement the vision. • Reinvigorate the change process with new projects and change agents.	• Declaring victory too soon—with the first performance improvement • Allowing resistors to convince "troops" that the war has been won
Institutionalize new approaches	• Articulate connections between new behaviors and corporate success. • Create leadership development and succession plans consistent with the new approach.	• Not creating new social norms and shared values consistent with changes • Promoting people into leadership positions who don't personify the new approach

performance. They focus on the potential revenue drop when an important patent expires, the five-year trend in declining margins in a core business, or an emerging market that everyone seems to be ignoring. They then find ways to communicate this information broadly and dramatically, especially with respect to crises, potential crises, or great opportunities that are very timely.

This first step is essential because just getting a transformation program started requires the aggressive cooperation of many individuals. Without motivation, people won't help, and the effort goes nowhere.

Compared with other steps in the change process, phase one can sound easy. It is not. Well over 50% of the companies I have watched fail in this first phase. What are the reasons for that failure? Sometimes executives underestimate how hard it can be to drive people out of their comfort zones. Sometimes they grossly overestimate how successful they have already been in increasing urgency. Sometimes they lack patience: "Enough with the preliminaries; let's get on with it." In many cases, executives become paralyzed by the downside possibilities. They worry that employees with seniority will become defensive, that morale will drop, that events will spin out of control, that short-term business results will be jeopardized, that the stock will sink, and that they will be blamed for creating a crisis.

A paralyzed senior management often comes from having too many managers and not enough leaders. Management's mandate is to minimize risk and to keep the current system operating. Change, by definition, requires creating a new system, which in turn always demands leadership. Phase one in a renewal process typically goes nowhere until enough real leaders are promoted or hired into senior-level jobs.

Transformations often begin, and begin well, when an organization has a new head who is a good leader and who sees the need for a major change. If the renewal target is the entire company, the CEO is key. If change is needed in a division, the division general manager is key. When these individuals are not new leaders, great leaders, or change champions, phase one can be a huge challenge.

Bad business results are both a blessing and a curse in the first phase. On the positive side, losing money does catch people's attention. But it also gives less maneuvering room. With good business results, the opposite is true: Convincing people of the need for change is much harder, but you have more resources to help make changes.

But whether the starting point is good performance or bad, in the more successful cases I have witnessed, an individual or a group always facilitates a frank discussion of potentially unpleasant facts about new competition, shrinking margins, decreasing market share, flat earnings, a lack of revenue growth, or other relevant indices of a declining competitive position. Because there seems to be an almost universal human tendency to shoot the bearer of bad news, especially if the head of the organization is not a change champion, executives in these companies often rely on outsiders to bring unwanted information. Wall Street analysts, customers, and consultants can all be helpful in this regard. The purpose of all this activity, in the words of one former CEO of a large European company, is "to make the status quo seem more dangerous than launching into the unknown."

In a few of the most successful cases, a group has manufactured a crisis. One CEO deliberately engineered the largest accounting loss in the company's history, creating huge pressures from Wall Street in the process. One division president commissioned first-ever customer satisfaction surveys, knowing full well that the results would be terrible. He then made these findings public. On the surface, such moves can look unduly risky. But there is also risk in playing it too safe: When the urgency rate is not pumped up enough, the transformation process cannot succeed, and the long-term future of the organization is put in jeopardy.

When is the urgency rate high enough? From what I have seen, the answer is when about 75% of a company's management is honestly convinced that business as usual is totally unacceptable. Anything less can produce very serious problems later on in the process.

Error 2: Not Creating a Powerful Enough Guiding Coalition

Major renewal programs often start with just one or two people. In cases of successful transformation efforts, the leadership coalition grows and grows over time. But whenever some minimum mass is not achieved early in the effort, nothing much worthwhile happens.

It is often said that major change is impossible unless the head of the organization is an active supporter. What I am talking about goes far beyond that. In successful transformations, the chairman or president or division general manager, plus another five or 15 or 50 people, come together and develop a shared commitment to excellent performance through renewal. In my experience, this group never includes all of the company's most senior executives because some people just won't buy in, at least not at first. But in the most successful cases, the coalition is always pretty powerful—in terms of titles, information and expertise, reputations, and relationships.

In both small and large organizations, a successful guiding team may consist of only three to five people during the first year of a renewal effort. But in big companies, the coalition needs to grow to the 20 to 50 range before much progress can be made in phase three and beyond. Senior managers always form the core of the group. But sometimes you find board members, a representative from a key customer, or even a powerful union leader.

Because the guiding coalition includes members who are not part of senior management, it tends to operate outside of the normal hierarchy by definition. This can be awkward, but it is clearly necessary. If the existing hierarchy were working well, there would be no need for a major transformation. But since the current system is not working, reform generally demands activity outside of formal boundaries, expectations, and protocol.

A high sense of urgency within the managerial ranks helps enormously in putting a guiding coalition together. But more is usually required. Someone needs to get these people together, help them develop a shared assessment of their company's problems and opportunities, and create a minimum level of trust and communication. Off-site retreats, for two or three days, are one popular vehicle for accomplishing this task. I have seen many groups of five to 35 executives attend a series of these retreats over a period of months.

Companies that fail in phase two usually underestimate the difficulties of producing change and thus the importance of a powerful guiding coalition. Sometimes they have no history of teamwork at the top and therefore undervalue the importance of this type of coalition. Sometimes they expect the team to be led by a staff executive from human resources, quality, or strategic planning instead of a key line manager. No matter how capable or dedicated the staff head, groups without strong line leadership never achieve the power that is required.

Efforts that don't have a powerful enough guiding coalition can make apparent progress for a while. But, sooner or later, the opposition gathers itself together and stops the change.

Error 3: Lacking a Vision

In every successful transformation effort that I have seen, the guiding coalition develops a picture of the future that is relatively easy to communicate and appeals to customers, stockholders, and employees. A vision always goes beyond the numbers that are typically found in five-year plans. A vision says something that helps clarify the direction in which an organization needs to move. Sometimes the first draft comes mostly from a single individual. It is usually a bit blurry, at least initially. But after the coalition works at it for three or five or even 12 months, something much better emerges through their tough analytical thinking and a little dreaming. Eventually, a strategy for achieving that vision is also developed.

In one midsize European company, the first pass at a vision contained two-thirds of the basic ideas that were in the final product. The concept of global reach was in the initial version from the beginning. So was the idea of becoming preeminent in certain businesses. But one central idea in the final version—getting out of low value-added activities—came only after a series of discussions over a period of several months.

Without a sensible vision, a transformation effort can easily dissolve into a list of confusing and incompatible projects that can take the organization in the wrong direction or nowhere at all. Without a sound vision, the reengineering project in the accounting department, the new 360-degree performance appraisal from the human resources department, the plant's quality program, the cultural change project in the sales force will not add up in a meaningful way.

In failed transformations, you often find plenty of plans, directives, and programs but no vision. In one case, a company gave out four-inch-thick notebooks describing its change effort. In mind-numbing detail, the books spelled out procedures, goals, methods, and deadlines. But nowhere was there a clear and compelling statement of where all this was leading. Not surprisingly, most of the employees with whom I talked were either confused or alienated. The big, thick books did not rally them together or inspire change. In fact, they probably had just the opposite effect.

In a few of the less successful cases that I have seen, management had a sense of direction, but it was too complicated or blurry to be useful. Recently, I asked an executive in a midsize company to describe his vision and received in return a barely comprehensible 30-minute lecture. Buried in his answer were the basic elements of a sound vision. But they were buried—deeply.

A useful rule of thumb: If you can't communicate the vision to someone in five minutes or less and get a reaction that signifies both understanding and interest, you are not yet done with this phase of the transformation process.

Error 4: Undercommunicating the Vision by a Factor of Ten

I've seen three patterns with respect to communication, all very common. In the first, a group actually does develop a pretty good transformation vision and then proceeds to communicate it by holding a single meeting or sending out a single communication. Having used about 0.0001% of the yearly intracompany communication, the group is startled when few people seem to understand the new approach. In the second pattern, the head of the organization spends a considerable amount of time making speeches to employee groups, but most people still don't get it (not surprising, since vision captures only 0.0005% of the total yearly communication). In the third pattern, much more effort goes into newsletters and speeches, but some very visible senior executives still behave in ways that are antithetical to the vision. The net result is that cynicism among the troops goes up, while belief in the communication goes down.

Transformation is impossible unless hundreds or thousands of people are willing to help, often to the point of making short-term sacrifices. Employees will not make sacrifices, even if they are unhappy with the status quo, unless they believe that useful change is possible. Without credible communication, and a lot of it, the hearts and minds of the troops are never captured.

This fourth phase is particularly challenging if the short-term sacrifices include job losses. Gaining understanding and support is tough when downsizing is a part of the vision. For this reason, successful visions usually include new growth possibilities and the commitment to treat fairly anyone who is laid off.

Executives who communicate well incorporate messages into their hour-by-hour activities. In a routine discussion about a business problem, they talk about how proposed solutions fit (or don't fit) into the bigger picture. In a regular performance appraisal, they talk about how the employee's behavior helps or undermines the vision. In a review of a division's quarterly performance, they talk not only about the numbers but also about how the division's executives are contributing to the transformation. In a routine Q&A with employees at a company facility, they tie their answers back to renewal goals.

In more successful transformation efforts, executives use all existing communication channels to broadcast the vision. They turn boring, unread company newsletters into lively articles about the vision. They take ritualistic, tedious quarterly management meetings and turn them into exciting discussions of the transformation. They throw out much of the company's generic management education and replace it with courses that focus on business problems and the new vision. The guiding principle is simple: Use every possible channel, especially those that are being wasted on nonessential information.

Perhaps even more important, most of the executives I have known in successful cases of major change learn to "walk the talk." They consciously attempt to become a living symbol of the new corporate culture. This is often not easy. A 60-year-old plant manager who has spent precious little time over 40 years thinking about customers will not suddenly behave in a customer-oriented way. But I have witnessed just such a person change, and change a great deal. In that case, a high level of urgency helped. The fact that the man was a part of the guiding coalition and the vision-creation team also helped. So did all the communication, which kept reminding him of the desired behavior, and all the feedback from his peers and subordinates, which helped him see when he was not engaging in that behavior.

Communication comes in both words and deeds, and the latter are often the most powerful form. Nothing undermines change more than behavior by important individuals that is inconsistent with their words.

Error 5: Not Removing Obstacles to the New Vision

Successful transformations begin to involve large numbers of people as the process progresses. Employees are emboldened to try new approaches, to develop new ideas, and to provide leadership. The only constraint is that the actions fit within the broad parameters of the overall vision. The more people involved, the better the outcome.

To some degree, a guiding coalition empowers others to take action simply by successfully communicating the new direction. But communication is never sufficient by itself. Renewal also requires the removal of obstacles. Too often, an employee understands the new vision and wants to help make it happen, but an elephant appears to be blocking the path. In some cases, the elephant is in the person's head, and the challenge is to convince the individual that no external obstacle exists. But in most cases, the blockers are very real.

Sometimes the obstacle is the organizational structure: Narrow job categories can seriously undermine efforts to increase productivity or make it very difficult even to think about customers. Sometimes compensation or performance-appraisal systems make people choose between the new vision and their own self-interest. Perhaps worst of all are bosses who refuse to change and who make demands that are inconsistent with the overall effort.

One company began its transformation process with much publicity and actually made good progress through the fourth phase. Then the change effort ground to a halt because the officer in charge of the company's largest division was allowed to undermine most of the new initiatives. He paid lip service to the process but did not change his behavior or encourage his managers to change. He did not reward the unconventional ideas called for in the vision. He allowed human resource systems to remain intact even when they were clearly inconsistent with the new ideals. I think the officer's motives were complex. To some degree, he did not believe the company needed major change. To some degree, he felt personally threatened by all the change. To some degree, he was afraid that he could not produce both change and the expected operating profit. But despite the fact that they backed the renewal effort, the other officers did virtually nothing to stop the one blocker. Again, the reasons were complex. The company had no history of confronting problems like this. Some people were afraid of the officer. The CEO was concerned that he might lose a talented executive. The net result was disastrous. Lower-level managers concluded that senior management had lied to them about their commitment to renewal, cynicism grew, and the whole effort collapsed.

In the first half of a transformation, no organization has the momentum, power, or time to get rid of all obstacles. But the big ones must be confronted and removed. If the blocker is a person, it is important that he or she be treated fairly and in a way that is consistent with the new vision. Action is essential, both to empower others and to maintain the credibility of the change effort as a whole.

Error 6: Not Systematically Planning for, and Creating, Short-Term Wins

Real transformation takes time, and a renewal effort risks losing momentum if there are no short-term goals to meet and celebrate. Most people won't go on the long march unless they see compelling evidence in 12 to 24 months that the journey is producing expected results. Without short-term wins, too many people give up or actively join the ranks of those people who have been resisting change.

One to two years into a successful transformation effort, you find quality beginning to go up on certain indices or the decline in net income stopping. You find some successful new product introductions or an upward shift in market share. You find an impressive productivity improvement or a statistically higher customer satisfaction rating. But whatever the case, the win is unambiguous. The result is not just a judgment call that can be discounted by those opposing change.

Creating short-term wins is different from hoping for short-term wins. The latter is passive, the former active. In a successful transformation, managers actively look for ways to obtain clear performance improvements, establish goals in the yearly planning system, achieve the objectives, and reward the people involved with recognition, promotions, and even money. For example, the guiding coalition at a U.S. manufacturing company produced a highly visible and successful new product introduction about 20 months after the start of its renewal effort. The new product was selected about six months into the effort because it met multiple criteria: It could be designed and launched in a relatively short period, it could be handled by a small team of people who were devoted to the new vision, it had upside potential, and the new product-development team could operate outside the established departmental structure without practical problems. Little was left to chance, and the win boosted the credibility of the renewal process.

Managers often complain about being forced to produce short-term wins, but I've found that pressure can be a useful element in a change effort. When it becomes clear to people that major change will take a long time, urgency levels can drop. Commitments to produce short-term wins help keep the urgency level up and force detailed analytical thinking that can clarify or revise visions.

Error 7: Declaring Victory Too Soon

After a few years of hard work, managers may be tempted to declare victory with the first clear performance improvement. While celebrating a win is fine, declaring the war won can be catastrophic. Until changes sink deeply into a company's culture, a process that can take five to ten years, new approaches are fragile and subject to regression.

In the recent past, I have watched a dozen change efforts operate under the reengineering theme. In all but two cases, victory was declared and the expensive consultants were paid and thanked when the first major project was completed after two to three years. Within two more years, the useful changes that had been introduced slowly disappeared. In two of the ten cases, it's hard to find any trace of the reengineering work today.

Over the past 20 years, I've seen the same sort of thing happen to huge quality projects, organizational development efforts, and more. Typically, the problems start early in the process: The urgency level is not intense enough, the guiding coalition is not powerful enough, and the vision is not clear enough. But it is the premature victory celebration that kills momentum. And then the powerful forces associated with tradition take over.

Ironically, it is often a combination of change initiators and change resistors that creates the premature victory celebration. In their enthusiasm over a clear sign of progress, the initiators go overboard. They are then joined by resistors, who are quick to spot any opportunity to stop change. After the celebration is over, the resistors point to the victory as a sign that the war has been won and the troops should be sent home. Weary troops allow themselves to be convinced that they won. Once home, the foot soldiers are reluctant to climb back on the ships. Soon thereafter, change comes to a halt, and tradition creeps back in.

Instead of declaring victory, leaders of successful efforts use the credibility afforded by short-term wins to tackle even bigger problems. They go after systems and structures that are not consistent with the transformation vision and have not been confronted before. They pay great attention to who is promoted, who is hired, and how people are developed. They include new reengineering projects that are even bigger in scope than the initial ones. They understand that renewal efforts take not months but years. In fact, in one of the most successful transformations that I have ever seen, we quantified the amount of change that occurred each year over a seven-year period. On a scale of one (low) to ten (high), year one received a two, year two a four, year three a three, year four a seven, year five an eight, year six a four, and year seven a two. The peak came in year five, fully 36 months after the first set of visible wins.

Error 8: Not Anchoring Changes in the Corporation's Culture

In the final analysis, change sticks when it becomes "the way we do things around here," when it seeps into the bloodstream of the corporate body. Until new behaviors are rooted in social norms and shared values, they are subject to degradation as soon as the pressure for change is removed.

Two factors are particularly important in institutionalizing change in corporate culture. The first is a conscious attempt to show people how the new approaches, behaviors, and attitudes have helped improve performance. When people are left on their own to make the connections, they sometimes create very inaccurate links. For example, because results improved while charismatic Harry was boss, the troops link his mostly idiosyncratic style with those results instead of seeing how their own improved customer service and productivity were instrumental. Helping people see the right connections requires communication. Indeed, one company was relentless, and it paid off enormously. Time was spent at every major management meeting to discuss why performance was increasing. The company newspaper ran article after article showing how changes had boosted earnings.

The second factor is taking sufficient time to make sure that the next generation of top management really does personify the new approach. If the requirements for promotion don't change, renewal rarely lasts. One bad succession decision at the top of an organization can undermine a decade of hard work. Poor succession decisions are possible when boards of directors are not an integral part of the renewal effort. In at least three instances I have seen, the champion for change was the retiring executive, and although his successor was not a resistor, he was not a change champion. Because the boards did not understand the transformations in any detail, they could not see that their choices were not good fits. The retiring executive in one case tried unsuccessfully to talk his board into a less seasoned candidate who better personified the transformation. In the other two cases, the CEOs did not resist the boards' choices, because they felt the transformation could not be undone by their successors. They were wrong. Within two years, signs of renewal began to disappear at both companies.

There are still more mistakes that people make, but these eight are the big ones. I realize that in a short article everything is made to sound a bit too simplistic. In reality, even successful change efforts are messy and full of surprises. But just as a relatively simple vision is needed to guide people through a major change, so a vision of the change process can reduce the error rate. And fewer errors can spell the difference between success and failure.

Originally published in March 1995. Reprint R0701J

Reinventing Your Business Model

by Mark W. Johnson, Clayton M. Christensen, and Henning Kagermann

IN 2003, APPLE INTRODUCED the iPod with the iTunes store, revolutionizing portable entertainment, creating a new market, and transforming the company. In just three years, the iPod/iTunes combination became a nearly $10 billion product, accounting for almost 50% of Apple's revenue. Apple's market capitalization catapulted from around $1 billion in early 2003 to over $150 billion by late 2007.

This success story is well known; what's less well known is that Apple was not the first to bring digital music players to market. A company called Diamond Multimedia introduced the Rio in 1998. Another firm, Best Data, introduced the Cabo 64 in 2000. Both products worked well and were portable and stylish. So why did the iPod, rather than the Rio or Cabo, succeed?

Apple did something far smarter than take a good technology and wrap it in a snazzy design. It took a good technology and wrapped it in a great business model. Apple's true innovation was to make downloading digital music easy and convenient. To do that, the company built a groundbreaking business model that combined hardware, software, and service. This approach worked like Gillette's famous blades-and-razor model in reverse: Apple essentially gave away the "blades" (low-margin iTunes music) to lock in purchase of the "razor" (the high-margin iPod). That model defined value in a new way and provided game-changing convenience to the consumer.

Business model innovations have reshaped entire industries and redistributed billions of dollars of value. Retail discounters such as Wal-Mart and Target, which entered the market with pioneering business models, now account for 75% of the total valuation of the retail sector. Low-cost U.S. airlines grew from a blip on the radar screen to 55% of the market value of all carriers. Fully 11 of the 27 companies born in the last quarter century that grew their way into the *Fortune* 500 in the past 10 years did so through business model innovation.

Stories of business model innovation from well-established companies like Apple, however, are rare. An analysis of major innovations within existing corporations in the past decade shows that precious few have been business-model related. And a recent American Management Association study determined that no more than 10% of innovation investment at global companies is focused on developing new business models.

Yet everyone's talking about it. A 2005 survey by the Economist Intelligence Unit reported that over 50% of executives believe business model innovation will become even more important for success than product or service innovation. A 2008 IBM survey of corporate CEOs echoed these results. Nearly all of the CEOs polled reported the need to adapt their business models; more than two-thirds said that extensive changes were required. And in these tough economic times, some CEOs are already looking to business model innovation to address permanent shifts in their market landscapes.

Senior managers at incumbent companies thus confront a frustrating question: Why is it so difficult to pull off the new growth that business model innovation can bring? Our research suggests two problems. The first is a lack of definition: Very little formal study has been done into the dynamics and processes of business model development. Second, few companies understand their existing business model well enough—the premise behind its development, its natural interdependencies, and its strengths and limitations. So they don't know when they can leverage their core business and when success requires a new business model.

After tackling these problems with dozens of companies, we have found that new business models often look unattractive to

Idea in Brief

When Apple introduced the iPod, it did something far smarter than wrap a good technology in a snazzy design. It wrapped a good technology in a **great business model**. Combining hardware, software, and service, the model provided game-changing convenience for consumers *and* record-breaking profits for Apple.

Great business models can reshape industries and drive spectacular growth. Yet many companies find business-model innovation difficult. Managers don't understand their existing model well enough to know when it needs changing—or how.

To determine whether your firm should alter its business model, Johnson, Christensen, and Kagermann advise these steps:

1. Articulate what makes your existing model successful. For example, what customer problem does it solve? How does it make money for your firm?

2. Watch for signals that your model needs changing, such as tough new competitors on the horizon.

3. Decide whether reinventing your model is worth the effort. The answer's yes only if the new model changes the industry or market.

internal and external stakeholders—at the outset. To see past the borders of what is and into the land of the new, companies need a road map.

Ours consists of three simple steps. The first is to realize that success starts by not thinking about business models at all. It starts with thinking about the opportunity to satisfy a real customer who needs a job done. The second step is to construct a blueprint laying out how your company will fulfill that need at a profit. In our model, that plan has four elements. The third is to compare that model to your existing model to see how much you'd have to change it to capture the opportunity. Once you do, you will know if you can use your existing model and organization or need to separate out a new unit to execute a new model. Every successful company is already fulfilling a real customer need with an effective business model, whether that model is explicitly understood or not. Let's take a look at what that entails.

Idea in Practice

Understand Your Current Business Model

A successful model has these components:

- **Customer value proposition.** The model helps customers perform a specific "job" that alternative offerings don't address.

  Example: MinuteClinics enable people to visit a doctor's office without appointments by making nurse practitioners available to treat minor health issues.

- **Profit formula.** The model generates value for your company through factors such as revenue model, cost structure, margins, and inventory turnover.

  Example: The Tata Group's inexpensive car, the Nano, is profitable because the company has reduced many cost structure elements, accepted lower-than-standard gross margins, and sold the Nano in large volumes to its target

market: first-time car buyers in emerging markets.

- **Key resources and processes.** Your company has the people, technology, products, facilities, equipment, and brand required to deliver the value proposition to your targeted customers. And it has processes (training, manufacturing, service) to leverage those resources.

  Example: For Tata Motors to fulfill the requirements of the Nano's profit formula, it had to reconceive how a car is designed, manufactured, and distributed. It redefined its supplier strategy, choosing to outsource a remarkable 85% of the Nano's components and to use nearly 60% fewer vendors than normal to reduce transaction costs.

Identify When a New Model May Be Needed

These circumstances often require business model change:

Business Model: A Definition

A business model, from our point of view, consists of four interlocking elements that, taken together, create and deliver value. The most important to get right, by far, is the first.

Customer value proposition (CVP)

A successful company is one that has found a way to create value for customers—that is, a way to help customers get an important job done. By "job" we mean a fundamental problem in a given situation that needs a solution. Once we understand the job and all its

An opportunity to . . .	Example
Address needs of large groups who find existing solutions too expensive or complicated.	The Nano's goal is to open car ownership to low-income consumers in emerging markets.
Capitalize on new technology, or leverage existing technologies in new markets.	A company develops a commercial application for a technology originally developed for military use.
Bring a job-to-be-done focus where it doesn't exist.	FedEx focused on performing customers' unmet "job": Receive packages faster and more reliably than any other service could.

A need to . . .	Example
Fend off low-end disruptors.	Mini-mills threatened the integrated steel mills a generation ago by making steel at significantly lower prices.
Respond to shifts in competition.	Power-tool maker Hilti switched from selling to renting its tools in part because "good enough" low-end entrants had begun chipping away at the market for selling high-quality tools.

dimensions, including the full process for how to get it done, we can design the offering. The more important the job is to the customer, the lower the level of customer satisfaction with current options for getting the job done, and the better your solution is than existing alternatives at getting the job done (and, of course, the lower the price), the greater the CVP. Opportunities for creating a CVP are at their most potent, we have found, when alternative products and services have not been designed with the real job in mind and you can design an offering that gets that job—and only that job—done perfectly. We'll come back to that point later.

Profit formula

The profit formula is the blueprint that defines how the company creates value for itself while providing value to the customer. It consists of the following:

- *Revenue model:* price x volume

- *Cost structure:* direct costs, indirect costs, economies of scale. Cost structure will be predominantly driven by the cost of the key resources required by the business model.

- *Margin model:* given the expected volume and cost structure, the contribution needed from each transaction to achieve desired profits.

- *Resource velocity:* how fast we need to turn over inventory, fixed assets, and other assets—and, overall, how well we need to utilize resources—to support our expected volume and achieve our anticipated profits.

People often think the terms "profit formulas" and "business models" are interchangeable. But how you make a profit is only one piece of the model. We've found it most useful to start by setting the price required to deliver the CVP and then work backwards from there to determine what the variable costs and gross margins must be. This then determines what the scale and resource velocity needs to be to achieve the desired profits.

Key resources

The key resources are assets such as the people, technology, products, facilities, equipment, channels, and brand required to deliver the value proposition to the targeted customer. The focus here is on the *key* elements that create value for the customer and the company, and the way those elements interact. (Every company also has generic resources that do not create competitive differentiation.)

Key processes

Successful companies have operational and managerial processes that allow them to deliver value in a way they can successfully repeat and increase in scale. These may include such recurrent tasks as training, development, manufacturing, budgeting, planning, sales, and service. Key processes also include a company's rules, metrics, and norms.

These four elements form the building blocks of any business. The customer value proposition and the profit formula define value for the customer and the company, respectively; key resources and key processes describe how that value will be delivered to both the customer and the company.

As simple as this framework may seem, its power lies in the complex interdependencies of its parts. Major changes to any of these four elements affect the others and the whole. Successful businesses devise a more or less stable system in which these elements bond to one another in consistent and complementary ways.

How Great Models Are Built

To illustrate the elements of our business model framework, we will look at what's behind two companies' game-changing business model innovations.

Creating a customer value proposition

It's not possible to invent or reinvent a business model without first identifying a clear customer value proposition. Often, it starts as a quite simple realization. Imagine, for a moment, that you are standing on a Mumbai road on a rainy day. You notice the large number of motor scooters snaking precariously in and out around the cars. As you look more closely, you see that most bear whole families—both parents and several children. Your first thought might be "That's crazy!" or "That's the way it is in developing countries—people get by as best they can."

The Elements of a Successful
Business Model

EVERY SUCCESSFUL COMPANY ALREADY operates according to an effective business model. By systematically identifying all of its constituent parts, executives can understand how the model fulfills a potent value proposition in a profitable way using certain key resources and key processes. With that understanding, they can then judge how well the same model could be used to fulfill a radically different CVP—and what they'd need to do to construct a new one, if need be, to capitalize on that opportunity.

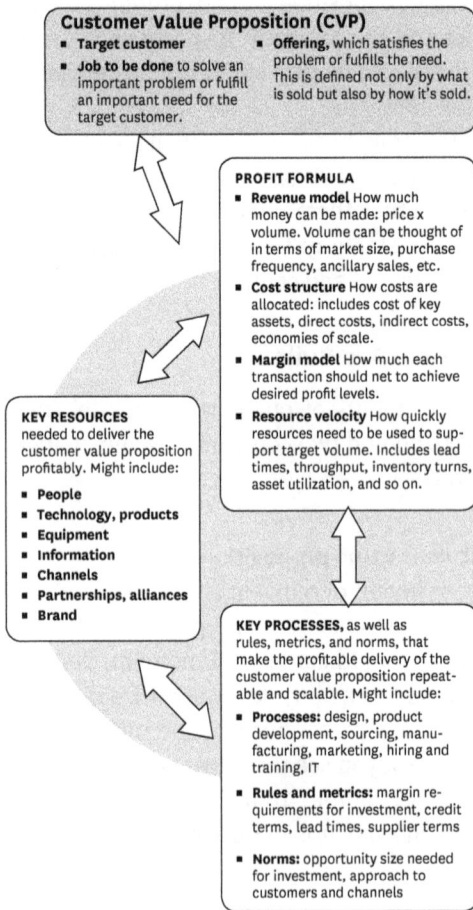

Customer Value Proposition (CVP)
- **Target customer**
- **Job to be done** to solve an important problem or fulfill an important need for the target customer.
- **Offering,** which satisfies the problem or fulfills the need. This is defined not only by what is sold but also by how it's sold.

PROFIT FORMULA
- **Revenue model** How much money can be made: price x volume. Volume can be thought of in terms of market size, purchase frequency, ancillary sales, etc.
- **Cost structure** How costs are allocated: includes cost of key assets, direct costs, indirect costs, economies of scale.
- **Margin model** How much each transaction should net to achieve desired profit levels.
- **Resource velocity** How quickly resources need to be used to support target volume. Includes lead times, throughput, inventory turns, asset utilization, and so on.

KEY RESOURCES needed to deliver the customer value proposition profitably. Might include:
- **People**
- **Technology, products**
- **Equipment**
- **Information**
- **Channels**
- **Partnerships, alliances**
- **Brand**

KEY PROCESSES, as well as rules, metrics, and norms, that make the profitable delivery of the customer value proposition repeatable and scalable. Might include:
- **Processes:** design, product development, sourcing, manufacturing, marketing, hiring and training, IT
- **Rules and metrics:** margin requirements for investment, credit terms, lead times, supplier terms
- **Norms:** opportunity size needed for investment, approach to customers and channels

When Ratan Tata of Tata Group looked out over this scene, he saw a critical job to be done: providing a safer alternative for scooter families. He understood that the cheapest car available in India cost easily five times what a scooter did and that many of these families could not afford one. Offering an affordable, safer, all-weather alternative for scooter families was a powerful value proposition, one with the potential to reach tens of millions of people who were not yet part of the car-buying market. Ratan Tata also recognized that Tata Motors' business model could not be used to develop such a product at the needed price point.

At the other end of the market spectrum, Hilti, a Liechtenstein-based manufacturer of high-end power tools for the construction industry, reconsidered the real job to be done for many of its current customers. A contractor makes money by finishing projects; if the required tools aren't available and functioning properly, the job doesn't get done. Contractors don't make money by *owning* tools; they make it by using them as efficiently as possible. Hilti could help contractors get the job done by selling tool *use* instead of the tools themselves—managing its customers' tool inventory by providing the best tool at the right time and quickly furnishing tool repairs, replacements, and upgrades, all for a monthly fee. To deliver on that value proposition, the company needed to create a fleet-management program for tools and in the process shift its focus from manufacturing and distribution to service. That meant Hilti had to construct a new profit formula and develop new resources and new processes.

The most important attribute of a customer value proposition is its precision: how perfectly it nails the customer job to be done—and nothing else. But such precision is often the most difficult thing to achieve. Companies trying to create the new often neglect to focus on *one* job; they dilute their efforts by attempting to do lots of things. In doing lots of things, they do nothing *really* well.

One way to generate a precise customer value proposition is to think about the four most common barriers keeping people from getting particular jobs done: insufficient wealth, access, skill, or time. Software maker Intuit devised QuickBooks to fulfill small-business owners' need to avoid running out of cash. By fulfilling that job with greatly simplified accounting software, Intuit broke the *skills barrier* that kept untrained small-business owners from using more-complicated accounting packages. MinuteClinic, the drugstore-based basic health care provider, broke the *time barrier* that kept people from visiting a doctor's office with minor health issues by making nurse practitioners available without appointments.

Designing a profit formula

Ratan Tata knew the only way to get families off their scooters and into cars would be to break the *wealth barrier* by drastically decreasing the price of the car. "What if I can change the game and make a car for one lakh?" Tata wondered, envisioning a price point of around US$2,500, less than half the price of the cheapest car available. This, of course, had dramatic ramifications for the profit formula: It required both a significant drop in gross margins and a radical reduction in many elements of the cost structure. He knew, however, he could still make money if he could increase sales volume dramatically, and he knew that his target base of consumers was potentially huge.

For Hilti, moving to a contract management program required shifting assets from customers' balance sheets to its own and generating revenue through a lease/subscription model. For a monthly fee, customers could have a full complement of tools at their fingertips, with repair and maintenance included. This would require a fundamental shift in all major components of the profit formula: the revenue stream (pricing, the staging of payments, and how to think about volume), the cost structure (including added sales development and contract management costs), and the supporting margins and transaction velocity.

Identifying key resources and processes

Having articulated the value proposition for both the customer and the business, companies must then consider the key resources and processes needed to deliver that value. For a professional services firm, for example, the key resources are generally its people, and the key processes are naturally people related (training and

Hilti Sidesteps Commoditization

HILTI IS CAPITALIZING ON a game-changing opportunity to increase profitability by turning products into a service. Rather than sell tools (at lower and lower prices), it's selling a "just-the-tool-you-need-when-you-need-it, no-repair-or-storage-hassles" service. Such a radical change in customer value proposition required a shift in all parts of its business model.

Traditional power tool company		Hilti's tool fleet management service
Sales of industrial and professional power tools and accessories	**Customer value proposition**	Leasing a comprehensive fleet of tools to increase contractors's on-site productivity
Low margins, high inventory turnover	**Profit formula**	Higher margins; asset heavy; monthly payments for tool maintenance, repair, and replacement
Distribution channel, low-cost manufacturing plants in developing countries, R&D	**Key resources and processes**	Strong direct-sales approach, contract management, IT systems for inventory management and repair, warehousing

development, for instance). For a packaged goods company, strong brands and well-selected channel retailers might be the key resources, and associated brand-building and channel-management processes among the critical processes.

Oftentimes, it's not the individual resources and processes that make the difference but their relationship to one another. Companies will almost always need to integrate their key resources and processes in a unique way to get a job done perfectly for a set of customers. When they do, they almost always create enduring competitive advantage. Focusing first on the value proposition and the profit formula makes clear how those resources and processes need to interrelate. For example, most general hospitals offer a value proposition that might be described as, "We'll do anything for anybody." Being all things to all people requires these hospitals to have a vast collection of resources (specialists, equipment, and so on) that can't be knit together in any proprietary way. The result is not just a lack of differentiation but dissatisfaction.

By contrast, a hospital that focuses on a specific value proposition can integrate its resources and processes in a unique way that delights customers. National Jewish Health in Denver, for example, is organized around a focused value proposition we'd characterize as, "If you have a disease of the pulmonary system, bring it here. We'll define its root cause and prescribe an effective therapy." Narrowing its focus has allowed National Jewish to develop processes that integrate the ways in which its specialists and specialized equipment work together.

For Tata Motors to fulfill the requirements of its customer value proposition and profit formula for the Nano, it had to reconceive how a car is designed, manufactured, and distributed. Tata built a small team of fairly young engineers who would not, like the company's more-experienced designers, be influenced and constrained in their thinking by the automaker's existing profit formulas. This team dramatically minimized the number of parts in the vehicle, resulting in a significant cost saving. Tata also reconceived its supplier strategy, choosing to outsource a remarkable 85% of the Nano's components and use nearly 60% fewer vendors than normal to reduce transaction costs and achieve better economies of scale.

At the other end of the manufacturing line, Tata is envisioning an entirely new way of assembling and distributing its cars. The ultimate plan is to ship the modular components of the vehicles to a combined network of company-owned and independent entrepreneur-owned assembly plants, which will build them to order. The Nano will be designed, built, distributed, and serviced in a radically new way— one that could not be accomplished without a new business model. And while the jury is still out, Ratan Tata may solve a traffic safety problem in the process.

For Hilti, the greatest challenge lay in training its sales representatives to do a thoroughly new task. Fleet management is not a half-hour sale; it takes days, weeks, even months of meetings to persuade customers to buy a program instead of a product. Suddenly,

field reps accustomed to dealing with crew leaders and on-site purchasing managers in mobile trailers found themselves staring down
CEOs and CFOs across conference tables.

Additionally, leasing required new resources—new people,
more robust IT systems, and other new technologies—to design
and develop the appropriate packages and then come to an agreement on monthly payments. Hilti needed a process for maintaining large arsenals of tools more inexpensively and effectively
than its customers had. This required warehousing, an inventory management system, and a supply of replacement tools. On
the customer management side, Hilti developed a website that
enabled construction managers to view all the tools in their fleet
and their usage rates. With that information readily available, the
managers could easily handle the cost accounting associated with
those assets.

Rules, norms, and metrics are often the last element to emerge
in a developing business model. They may not be fully envisioned
until the new product or service has been road tested. Nor should
they be. Business models need to have the flexibility to change in
their early years.

When a New Business Model Is Needed

Established companies should not undertake business-model innovation lightly. They can often create new products that disrupt competitors without fundamentally changing their own business model.
Procter & Gamble, for example, developed a number of what it calls
"disruptive market innovations" with such products as the Swiffer
disposable mop and duster and Febreze, a new kind of air freshener.
Both innovations built on P&G's existing business model and its
established dominance in household consumables.

There are clearly times, however, when creating new growth
requires venturing not only into unknown market territory but also
into unknown business model territory. When? The short answer
is "When significant changes are needed to all four elements of
your existing model." But it's not always that simple. Management

judgment is clearly required. That said, we have observed five strategic circumstances that often require business model change:

1. The opportunity to address through disruptive innovation the needs of large groups of potential customers who are shut out of a market entirely because existing solutions are too expensive or complicated for them. This includes the opportunity to democratize products in emerging markets (or reach the bottom of the pyramid), as Tata's Nano does.

2. The opportunity to capitalize on a brand-new technology by wrapping a new business model around it (Apple and MP3 players) or the opportunity to leverage a tested technology by bringing it to a whole new market (say, by offering military technologies in the commercial space or vice versa).

3. The opportunity to bring a job-to-be-done focus where one does not yet exist. That's common in industries where companies focus on products or customer segments, which leads them to refine existing products more and more, increasing commoditization over time. A jobs focus allows companies to redefine industry profitability. For example, when FedEx entered the package delivery market, it did not try to compete through lower prices or better marketing. Instead, it concentrated on fulfilling an entirely unmet customer need to receive packages far, far faster, and more reliably, than any service then could. To do so, it had to integrate its key processes and resources in a vastly more efficient way. The business model that resulted from this job-to-be-done emphasis gave FedEx a significant competitive advantage that took UPS many years to copy.

4. The need to fend off low-end disrupters. If the Nano is successful, it will threaten other automobile makers, much as minimills threatened the integrated steel mills a generation ago by making steel at significantly lower cost.

5. The need to respond to a shifting basis of competition. Inevitably, what defines an acceptable solution in a market

Dow Corning Embraces the Low End

TRADITIONALLY HIGH-MARGIN DOW CORNING found new opportunities in low-margin offerings by setting up a separate business unit that operates in an entirely different way. By fundamentally differentiating its low-end and high-end offerings, the company avoided cannibalizing its traditional business even as it found new profits at the low end.

Established business		New business unit
Customized solutions, negotiated contracts	**Customer value proposition**	No frills, bulk prices, sold through the internet
High-margin, high-overhead retail prices pay for value-added services	**Profit formula**	Spot-market pricing, low overhead to accommodate lower margins, high throughput
R&D, sales, and services orientation	**Key resources and processes**	IT system, lowest-cost processes, maximum automation

will change over time, leading core market segments to commoditize. Hilti needed to change its business model in part because of lower global manufacturing costs; "good enough" low-end entrants had begun chipping away at the market for high-quality power tools.

Of course, companies should not pursue business model reinvention unless they are confident that the opportunity is large enough to warrant the effort. And, there's really no point in instituting a new business model unless it's not only new to the company but in some way new or game-changing to the industry or market. To do otherwise would be a waste of time and money.

These questions will help you evaluate whether the challenge of business model innovation will yield acceptable results. Answering "yes" to all four greatly increases the odds of successful execution:

- Can you nail the job with a focused, compelling customer value proposition?

- Can you devise a model in which all the elements—the customer value proposition, the profit formula, the key resources, and the key processes—work together to get the job done in the most efficient way possible?

- Can you create a new business development process unfettered by the often negative influences of your core business?

- Will the new business model disrupt competitors?

Creating a new model for a new business does not mean the current model is threatened or should be changed. A new model often reinforces and complements the core business, as Dow Corning discovered.

How Dow Corning Got Out of Its Own Way

When business model innovation is clearly called for, success lies not only in getting the model right but also in making sure the incumbent business doesn't in some way prevent the new model from creating value or thriving. That was a problem for Dow Corning when it built a new business unit—with a new profit formula—from scratch.

For many years, Dow Corning had sold thousands of silicone-based products and provided sophisticated technical services to an array of industries. After years of profitable growth, however, a number of product areas were stagnating. A strategic review uncovered a critical insight: Its low-end product segment was commoditizing. Many customers experienced in silicone application no longer needed technical services; they needed basic products at low prices. This shift created an opportunity for growth, but to exploit that opportunity Dow Corning had to figure out a way to serve these customers with a lower-priced product. The problem was that both the business model and the culture were built on high-priced, innovative product and service packages. In 2002, in pursuit of what was essentially a commodity business for low-end customers, Dow Corning CEO Gary Anderson asked executive Don Sheets to form a team to start a new business.

When the Old Model Will Work

YOU DON'T ALWAYS NEED a new business model to capitalize on a game-changing opportunity. Sometimes, as P&G did with its Swiffer, a company finds that its current model is revolutionary in a new market. When will the old model do? When you can fulfill the new customer value proposition:

- With your current profit formula
- Using most, if not all, of your current key resources and processes
- Using the same core metrics, rules, and norms you now use to run your business

---

The team began by formulating a customer value proposition that it believed would fulfill the job to be done for these price-driven customers. It determined that the price point had to drop 15% (which for a commoditizing material was a huge reduction). As the team analyzed what that new customer value proposition would require, it realized reaching that point was going to take a lot more than merely eliminating services. Dramatic price reduction would call for a different profit formula with a fundamentally lower cost structure, which depended heavily on developing a new IT system. To sell more products faster, the company would need to use the internet to automate processes and reduce overhead as much as possible.

Breaking the rules

As a mature and successful company, Dow Corning was full of highly trained employees used to delivering its high-touch, customized value proposition. To automate, the new business would have to be far more standardized, which meant instituting different and, overall, much stricter rules. For example, order sizes would be limited to a few, larger-volume options; order lead times would fall between two and four weeks (exceptions would cost extra); and credit terms would be fixed. There would be charges if a purchaser required customer service. The writing was on the wall: The new venture would be low-touch, self-service, and standardized. To succeed, Dow Corning would have to break the rules that had previously guided its success.

Sheets next had to determine whether this new venture, with its new rules, could succeed within the confines of Dow Corning's core enterprise. He set up an experimental war game to test how existing staff and systems would react to the requirements of the new customer value proposition. He got crushed as entrenched habits and existing processes thwarted any attempt to change the game. It became clear that the corporate antibodies would kill the initiative before it got off the ground. The way forward was clear: The new venture had to be free from existing rules and free to decide what rules would be appropriate in order for the new commodity line of business to thrive. To nurture the opportunity—and also protect the existing model—a new business unit with a new brand identity was needed. Xiameter was born.

Identifying new competencies

Following the articulation of the new customer value proposition and new profit formula, the Xiameter team focused on the new competencies it would need, its key resources and processes. Information technology, just a small part of Dow Corning's core competencies at that time, emerged as an essential part of the now web-enabled business. Xiameter also needed employees who could make smart decisions very quickly and who would thrive in a fast-changing environment, filled initially with lots of ambiguity. Clearly, new abilities would have to be brought into the business.

Although Xiameter would be established and run as a separate business unit, Don Sheets and the Xiameter team did not want to give up the incumbency advantage that deep knowledge of the industry and of their own products gave them. The challenge was to tap into the expertise without importing the old-rules mind-set. Sheets conducted a focused HR search within Dow Corning for risk takers. During the interview process, when he came across candidates with the right skills, he asked them to take the job on the spot, before they left the room. This approach allowed him to cherry-pick those who could make snap decisions and take big risks.

What Rules, Norms, and Metrics Are Standing in Your Way?

IN ANY BUSINESS, a fundamental understanding of the core model often fades into the mists of institutional memory, but it lives on in rules, norms, and metrics put in place to protect the status quo (for example, "Gross margins must be at 40%"). They are the first line of defense against any new model's taking root in an existing enterprise.

Financial

- Gross margins
- Opportunity size
- Unit pricing
- Unit margin
- Time to breakeven
- Net present value calculations
- Fixed cost investment
- Credit items

Operational

- End-product quality
- Supplier quality
- Owned versus outsourced manufacturing
- Customer service
- Channels
- Lead times
- Throughput

Other

- Pricing
- Performance demands
- Product-development life cycles
- Basis for individuals' rewards and incentives
- Brand parameters

The secret sauce: patience

Successful new businesses typically revise their business models four times or so on the road to profitability. While a well-considered business-model-innovation process can often shorten this cycle, successful incumbents must tolerate initial failure and grasp the need for course correction. In effect, companies have to focus on learning and adjusting as much as on executing. We recommend companies with new business models be patient for growth (to allow the market opportunity to unfold) but impatient for profit (as an early validation that the model works). A profitable business is the best early indication of a viable model.

Accordingly, to allow for the trial and error that naturally accompanies the creation of the new while also constructing a development cycle that would produce results and demonstrate feasibility with minimal resource outlay, Dow Corning kept the scale of Xiameter's operation small but developed an aggressive timetable for launch and set the goal of becoming profitable by the end of year one.

Xiameter paid back Dow Corning's investment in just three months and went on to become a major, transformative success. Beforehand, Dow Corning had had no online sales component; now 30% of sales originate online, nearly three times the industry average. Most of these customers are new to the company. Far from cannibalizing existing customers, Xiameter has actually supported the main business, allowing Dow Corning's salespeople to more easily enforce premium pricing for their core offerings while providing a viable alternative for the price-conscious.

Established companies' attempts at transformative growth typically spring from product or technology innovations. Their efforts are often characterized by prolonged development cycles and fitful attempts to find a market. As the Apple iPod story that opened this article suggests, truly transformative businesses are never exclusively about the discovery and commercialization of a great technology. Their success comes from enveloping the new technology in an appropriate, powerful business model.

Bob Higgins, the founder and general partner of Highland Capital Partners, has seen his share of venture success and failure in his 20 years in the industry. He sums up the importance and power of business model innovation this way: "I think historically where we [venture capitalists] fail is when we back technology. Where we succeed is when we back new business models."

Originally published in December 2008. Reprint R0812C

Leadership
Is a Conversation

by Boris Groysberg and Michael Slind

THE COMMAND-AND-CONTROL APPROACH to management has in recent years become less and less viable. Globalization, new technologies, and changes in how companies create value and interact with customers have sharply reduced the efficacy of a purely directive, top-down model of leadership. What will take the place of that model? Part of the answer lies in how leaders manage communication within their organizations—that is, how they handle the flow of information to, from, and among their employees. Traditional corporate communication must give way to a process that is more dynamic and more sophisticated. Most important, that process must be *conversational.*

We arrived at that conclusion while conducting a recent research project that focused on the state of organizational communication in the 21st century. Over more than two years we interviewed professional communicators as well as top leaders at a variety of organizations—large and small, blue chip and start-up, for-profit and nonprofit, U.S. and international. To date we have spoken with nearly 150 people at more than 100 companies. Both implicitly and explicitly, participants in our research mentioned their efforts to "have a conversation" with their people or their ambition to "advance the conversation" within their companies. Building upon the insights and examples gleaned from this research, we have developed a model of leadership that we call "organizational conversation."

Elements of organizational conversation

Intimacy	Interactivity	Inclusion	Intentionality
How leaders relate to employees	*How leaders use communication channels*	*How leaders develop organizational content*	*How leaders convey strategy*
Old model: corporate communication			
Information flow is primarily top-down	Messages are broadcast to employees	Top executives create and control messaging	Communication is fragmented, reactive, and ad hoc
Tone is formal and corporate	Print newsletters, memos, and speeches predominate	Employees are passive consumers of information	Leaders use assertion to achieve strategic alignment
New model: organizational communication			
Communication is personal and direct	Leaders talk with employees, not to them	Leaders relinquish a measure of control over content	A clear agenda informs all communication
Leaders value trust and authenticity	Organizational culture fosters back-and-forth, face-to-face interaction	Employees actively participate in organizational messaging	Leaders carefully explain the agenda to employees
			Strategy emerges from a cross-organizational conversation
What it means for employers and employees			
Leaders emphasize listening to employees rather than just speaking to them	Leaders use video and social media tools to facilitate two-way communication	Leaders involve employees in telling the company story	Leaders build their messaging around company strategy
Employees engage in a bottom-up exchange of ideas	Employees interact with colleagues through blogs and discussion forums	Employees act as brand ambassadors and thought leaders	Employees take part in creating strategy via specially designed communication vehicles

Idea in Brief

One-way, top-down communication between leaders and their employees is no longer useful or even realistic.

Today's leaders achieve far more engagement and credibility when they take part in genuine conversation with the people who work for and with them. A conversation is a frank exchange of ideas and information with an implicit or explicit agenda.

Corporate conversation reflects a new reality: Thanks in part to digital and social technologies, employees have found a public voice. They'll use it whether their bosses like it or not.

The good news for leaders is that people can talk up a company in a way that's more interesting and attractive than any obvious public relations campaign.

Smart leaders today, we have found, engage with employees in a way that resembles an ordinary person-to-person conversation more than it does a series of commands from on high. Furthermore, they initiate practices and foster cultural norms that instill a conversational sensibility throughout their organizations. Chief among the benefits of this approach is that it allows a large or growing company to function like a small one. By talking with employees, rather than simply issuing orders, leaders can retain or recapture some of the qualities—operational flexibility, high levels of employee engagement, tight strategic alignment—that enable start-ups to outperform better-established rivals.

In developing our model, we have identified four elements of organizational conversation that reflect the essential attributes of interpersonal conversation: intimacy, interactivity, inclusion, and intentionality. Leaders who power their organizations through conversation-based practices need not (so to speak) dot all four of these i's. However, as we've discovered in our research, these elements tend to reinforce one another. In the end, they coalesce to form a single integrated process.

Intimacy: Getting Close

Personal conversation flourishes to the degree that the participants stay close to each other, figuratively as well as literally. Organizational conversation, similarly, requires leaders to minimize the distances—institutional, attitudinal, and sometimes spatial—that typically separate them from their employees. Where conversational intimacy prevails, those with decision-making authority seek and earn the trust (and hence the careful attention) of those who work under that authority. They do so by cultivating the art of listening to people at all levels of the organization and by learning to speak with employees directly and authentically. Physical proximity between leaders and employees isn't always feasible. Nor is it essential. What *is* essential is mental or emotional proximity. Conversationally adept leaders step down from their corporate perches and then step up to the challenge of communicating personally and transparently with their people.

This intimacy distinguishes organizational conversation from long-standard forms of corporate communication. It shifts the focus from a top-down distribution of information to a bottom-up exchange of ideas. It's less corporate in tone and more casual. And it's less about issuing and taking orders than about asking and answering questions.

Conversational intimacy can become manifest in various ways— among them gaining trust, listening well, and getting personal.

Gaining trust

Where there is no trust, there can be no intimacy. For all practical purposes, the reverse is true as well. No one will dive into a heart-felt exchange of views with someone who seems to have a hidden agenda or a hostile manner, and any discussion that does unfold between two people will be rewarding and substantive only to the extent that each person can take the other at face value.

But trust is hard to achieve. In organizations it has become especially difficult for employees to put trust in their leaders, who will earn it only if they are authentic and straightforward. That may mean addressing topics that feel off-limits, such as sensitive financial data.

Athenahealth, a medical-records technology provider, has gone as far as to treat every last one of its employees as an "insider" under the strict legal meaning of the term. Insiders are defined as employees entrusted with strategic and financial information that could materially affect the company's business prospects and hence its stock price—a status typically accorded only to top-tier officers. Opening the books to such a degree was a risky move, discouraged by the company's underwriters and frowned upon by the SEC. But Athenahealth's leaders wanted employees to become insiders in more than just the regulatory sense; they wanted them to be thoroughly involved in the business.

Listening well

Leaders who take organizational conversation seriously know when to stop talking and start listening. Few behaviors enhance conversational intimacy as much as attending to what people say. True attentiveness signals respect for people of all ranks and roles, a sense of curiosity, and even a degree of humility.

Duke Energy's president and CEO, James E. Rogers, instituted a series of what he called "listening sessions" when he was the CEO and chairman of Cinergy (which later merged with Duke). Meeting with groups of 90 to 100 managers in three-hour sessions, he invited participants to raise any pressing issues. Through these discussions he gleaned information that might otherwise have escaped his attention. At one session, for example, he heard from a group of supervisors about a problem related to uneven compensation. "You know how long it would have taken for that to bubble up in the organization?" he asks. Having heard directly from those affected by the problem, he could instruct his HR department to find a solution right away.

Getting personal

Rogers not only invited people to raise concerns about the company but also solicited feedback on his own performance. He asked employees at one session to grade him on a scale of A to F. The results, recorded anonymously, immediately appeared on a screen for all to see. The grades were generally good, but less than half of employees were willing to give him an A. He took the feedback seriously and began to conduct the exercise regularly. He also began asking open-ended questions about his performance. Somewhat ironically, he found that "internal communication" was the area in which the highest number of participants believed he had room for improvement. Even as Rogers sought to get close to employees by way of organizational conversation, a fifth of his people were urging him to get closer still. True listening involves taking the bad with the good, absorbing criticism even when it is direct and personal—and even when those delivering it work for you.

At Exelon, an energy provider headquartered in Chicago, a deeply personal form of organizational conversation emerged from a project aimed at bringing the company's corporate values alive for its employees. Values statements typically do little to instill intimacy; they're generally dismissed as just talk. So Exelon experimented in its communication about diversity, a core value: It used a series of short video clips—no fuss, no pretense, no high production values—of top leaders speaking unscripted, very personally, about what diversity meant to them. They talked about race, sexual orientation, and other issues that rarely go on the table in a corporation. Ian McLean, then an Exelon finance executive, spoke of growing up in Manchester, England, the son of a working-class family, and feeling the sting of class prejudice. Responding to a question about a time when he felt "different," he described going to work in a bank where most of his colleagues had upper-class backgrounds: "My accent was different. . . . I wasn't included, I wasn't invited, and I was made to think I wasn't quite as smart as they were. . . . I never want anyone else to feel that [way] around me." Such unadorned stories make a strong impression on employees.

Interactivity: Promoting Dialogue

A personal conversation, by definition, involves an exchange of comments and questions between two or more people. The sound of one person talking is not, obviously, a conversation. The same applies to organizational conversation, in which leaders talk *with* employees and not just *to* them. This interactivity makes the conversation open and fluid rather than closed and directive. It entails shunning the simplicity of monologue and embracing

The New Realities of Leadership Communication

FIVE LONG-TERM BUSINESS TRENDS are forcing the shift from corporate communication to organizational conversation.

Economic Change

As service industries have become more economically significant than manufacturing industries, and as knowledge work has supplanted other kinds of labor, the need for sophisticated ways to process and share information has grown more acute.

Organizational Change

As companies have become flatter and less hierarchical, and frontline employees more pivotally involved in value-creating work, lateral and bottom-up communication has achieved the importance of top-down communication.

Global Change

As workforces have become more diverse and more widely dispersed, navigating across cultural and geographic lines has required interactions that are fluid and complex.

Generational Change

As millennials and other younger workers have gained a foothold in organizations, they have expected peers and authority figures alike to communicate with them in a dynamic, two-way fashion.

Technological Change

As digital networks have made instant connectivity a norm of business life, and as social media platforms have grown more powerful and more ubiquitous, a reliance on older, less conversational channels of communication has ceased to be tenable.

---

the unpredictable vitality of dialogue. The pursuit of interactivity reinforces, and builds upon, intimacy: Efforts to close gaps between employees and their leaders will founder if employees don't have both the tools and the institutional support they need to speak up and (where appropriate) talk back.

In part, a shift toward greater interactivity reflects a shift in the use of communication channels. For decades, technology made it difficult or impossible to support interaction within organizations of any appreciable size. The media that companies used to achieve scale and efficiency in their communications—print and broadcast, in particular—operated in one direction only. But new channels have disrupted that one-way structure. Social technology gives leaders and their employees the ability to invest an organizational setting with the style and spirit of personal conversation.

Yet interactivity isn't just a matter of finding and deploying the right technology. Equally if not more important is the need to buttress social media with social *thinking*. Too often, an organization's prevailing culture works against any attempt to transform corporate communication into a two-way affair. For many executives and managers, the temptation to treat every medium at their disposal as if it were a megaphone has proved hard to resist. In some companies, however, leaders have fostered a genuinely interactive culture—values, norms, and behaviors that create a welcoming space for dialogue.

To see how interactivity works, consider Cisco Systems. As it happens, Cisco makes and sells various products that fall under the social technology umbrella. In using them internally, its people have explored the benefits of enabling high-quality back-and-forth communication. One such product, TelePresence, simulates an in-person meeting by beaming video feeds between locations. Multiple large screens create a wraparound effect, and specially designed meeting tables (in an ideal configuration) mirror one another so that users feel as if they were seated at the same piece of furniture. In one sense this is a more robust version of a web-based video chat, with none of the delays or hiccups that typically mar online video. More important, it masters the critical issue of visual scale. When Cisco engineers studied remote interactions, they found that if the on-screen image of a person is less than 80% of his or her true size, those who see the image are less engaged in talking with that person. TelePresence participants appear life-size and can look one another in the eye.

TelePresence is a sophisticated technology tool, but what it enables is the recovery of immediate, spontaneous give-and-take.

Randy Pond, Cisco's executive vice president of operations, processes, and systems, thinks this type of interaction offers the benefit of the "whole" conversation—a concept he illustrated for us with an anecdote. Sitting at his desk for a video conference one day, he could see video feeds of several colleagues on his computer screen when he made a comment to the group and a participant "just put his head in his hands"—presumably in dismay, and presumably not considering that Pond could see him. "I said, 'I can see you,'" Pond told us. "'If you disagree, *tell me.*'" Pond was then able to engage with his skeptical colleague to get the "whole story." A less interactive form of communication might have produced such information eventually—but far less efficiently.

At the crux of Cisco's communication culture is its CEO, John Chambers, who holds various forums to keep in touch with employees. About every other month, for instance, he leads a "birthday chat," open to any Cisco employee whose birthday falls in the relevant two-month period. Senior managers aren't invited, lest their presence keep attendees from speaking openly. Chambers also records a video blog about once a month—a brief, improvisational message delivered by e-mail to all employees. The use of video allows him to speak to his people directly, informally, and without a script; it suggests immediacy and builds trust. And despite the inherently one-way nature of a video blog, Chambers and his team have made it interactive by inviting video messages as well as text comments from employees.

Inclusion: Expanding Employees' Roles

At its best, personal conversation is an equal-opportunity endeavor. It enables participants to share ownership of the substance of their discussion. As a consequence, they can put their own ideas—and, indeed, their hearts and souls—into the conversational arena. Organizational conversation, by the same token, calls on employees to participate in generating the content that makes up a company's story. Inclusive leaders, by counting employees among a company's official or quasi-official communicators, turn those employees into full-fledged conversation partners. In the process, such leaders raise the level of emotional engagement that employees bring to company life in general.

Inclusion adds a critical dimension to the elements of intimacy and interactivity. Whereas intimacy involves the efforts of leaders to get closer to employees, inclusion focuses on the role that employees play in that process. It also extends the practice of interactivity by enabling employees to provide their own ideas—often on official company channels—rather than simply parrying the ideas that others present. It enables them to serve as frontline *content providers.*

In the standard corporate communication model, top executives and professional communicators monopolize the creation of content and keep a tight rein on what people write or say on official company channels. But when a spirit of inclusion takes hold, engaged employees can adopt important new roles, creating content themselves and acting as brand ambassadors, thought leaders, and storytellers.

Brand ambassadors

When employees feel passionate about their company's products and services, they become living representatives of the brand. This can and does happen organically—lots of people love what they do for a living and will talk it up on their own time. But some companies actively promote that kind of behavior. Coca-Cola, for instance, has created a formal ambassadorship program, aimed at encouraging employees to promote the Coke image and product line in speech and in practice. The Coke intranet provides resources such as a tool that connects employees to company-sponsored volunteer activities. The centerpiece of the program is a list of nine ambassadorial behaviors, which include helping the company "win at the point of sale" (by taking it on themselves to tidy store displays in retail outlets, for example), relaying sales leads, and reporting instances in which a retailer has run out of a Coke product.

Thought leaders

To achieve market leadership in a knowledge-based field, companies may rely on consultants or in-house professionals to draft speeches, articles, white papers, and the like. But often the most innovative thinking occurs deep within an organization, where people develop and test new products and services. Empowering those people to create and promote thought-leadership material can be a smart, quick way to bolster a company's reputation among key industry players. In recent years Juniper Networks has sponsored initiatives to get potential thought leaders out of their labs and offices and into public venues where industry experts and customers can watch them strut their intellectual stuff. The company's engineers are working on the next wave of systems silicon and hardware and can offer keen insights into trends. To communicate their perspective to relevant audiences, Juniper dispatches them to national and international technology conferences and arranges for them to meet with customers at company-run briefing centers.

Storytellers

People are accustomed to hearing corporate communication professionals tell stories about a company, but there's nothing like hearing a story direct from the front lines. When employees speak from their own experience, unedited, the message comes to life. The computer storage giant EMC actively elicits stories from its people. Leaders look to them for ideas on how to improve business performance and for thoughts about the company itself. The point is to instill the notion that ideas are welcome from all corners. As just one example, in 2009 the company published *The Working Mother Experience*—a 250-page coffee-table book written by and for EMCers on the topic of being both a successful EMC employee and a parent. The project, initiated at the front lines, was championed by Frank Hauck, then the executive vice president of global marketing and customer quality. It's not unusual for a big company like EMC to produce such a book as a vanity project, but this was no corporate communication effort; it was a peer-driven endeavor, led by employees. Several dozen EMCers also write blogs, many on public sites, expressing their unfiltered thoughts about life at the company and sharing their ideas about technology.

Of course, inclusion means that executives cede a fair amount of control over how the company is represented to the world. But the fact is that cultural and technological changes have eroded that control anyway. Whether you like it or not, anybody can tarnish (or polish) your company's reputation right from her cube, merely by e-mailing an internal document to a reporter, a blogger, or even a group of friends—or by posting her thoughts in an online forum. Thus inclusive leaders are making a virtue out of necessity. Scott Huennekens, the CEO of Volcano Corporation, suggests that a looser approach to communication has made organizational life less stifling and more productive than it used to be. The free flow of information creates a freer spirit. Some companies do try to set some basic expectations. Infosys, for instance, acknowledging its lack of control over employees' participation in social networks, tells employees that they may disagree but asks them not to be *disagreeable.*

And quite often, leaders have discovered, a system of self-regulation by employees fills the void left by top-down control. Somebody comes out with an outrageous statement, the community responds, and the overall sentiment swings back to the middle.

Intentionality: Pursuing an Agenda

A personal conversation, if it's truly rich and rewarding, will be open but not aimless; the participants will have some sense of what they hope to achieve. They might seek to entertain each other, or to persuade each other, or to learn from each other. In the absence of such intent, a conversation will either meander or run into a blind alley. Intent confers order and meaning on even the loosest and most digressive forms of chatter. That principle applies to organizational conversation, too. Over time, the many voices that contribute to the process of communication within a company must converge on a single vision of what that communication is *for.* To put it another way: The conversation that unfolds within a company should reflect a shared agenda that aligns with the company's strategic objectives.

Intentionality differs from the other three elements of organizational conversation in one key respect. While intimacy, interactivity, and inclusion all serve to open up the flow of information and ideas within a company, intentionality brings a measure of closure to that process: It enables leaders and employees to derive strategically relevant action from the push and pull of discussion and debate.

Conversational intentionality requires leaders to convey strategic principles not just by asserting them but by explaining them—by generating consent rather than commanding assent. In this new model, leaders speak extensively and explicitly with employees about the vision and the logic that underlie executive decision making. As a result, people at every level gain a big-picture view of where their company stands within its competitive environment. In short, they become *conversant* in matters of organizational strategy.

One way to help employees understand the company's governing strategy is to let them have a part in creating it. The leadership team at Infosys has taken to including a broad range of employees in the company's annual strategy-development process. In late 2009, as Infosys leaders began to build an organizational strategy for the 2011 fiscal year, they invited people from every rank and division of the company to join in. In particular, explains Kris Gopalakrishnan, a cofounder and executive cochairman, they asked employees to submit ideas on "the significant transformational trends that we see affecting our customers." Using those ideas, strategic planners at Infosys came up with a list of 17 trends, ranging from the growth of emerging markets to the increasing emphasis on environmental sustainability. They then created a series of online forums in which employees could suggest how to match each trend with various customer solutions that the company might offer. Technology and social networks enabled bottom-up participation across the company.

In 2008 Kingfisher plc, the world's third-largest home improvement retailer, began pursuing a new strategy to transform a group of historically discrete business units into "one team," in part through intentional organizational conversation. To launch the effort, company leaders held a three-day event in Barcelona for retail executives. On the second day everyone participated in a 90-minute session called Share at the Marketplace, which was intended to emulate a classic Mediterranean or Middle Eastern bazaar. One group of participants, called "suppliers," donned aprons, and each person stood at one of 22 stalls, ready to give a spiel about a business practice developed by people in his or her part of the Kingfisher organization. Essentially they were purveyors of ideas.

Another group—executive committee members—served as facilitators, ambling through the aisles and providing words of encouragement. The third and largest group acted as buyers, moving from one stall to the next, examining the "merchandise," and occasionally "purchasing" one of the ideas. Using special checkbooks issued for this purpose, buyers could draft up to five checks each to pay for suppliers' wares. Such transactions had no force beyond the confines of the session, but they conveyed a strong message to the suppliers: What you're telling me is impressive. The essence of the marketplace was the peer-to-peer sharing of best practices in an informal, messy, and noisy environment. But the idea was also to treat conversation as a means to an end—to use it to achieve strategic alignment across a diverse group of participants.

Conversation goes on in every company, whether you recognize it or not. That has always been the case, but today the conversation has the potential to spread well beyond your walls, and it's largely out of your control. Smart leaders find ways to use conversation—to manage the flow of information in an honest, open fashion. One-way broadcast messaging is a relic, and slick marketing materials have as little effect on employees as they do on customers. But people will listen to communication that is intimate, interactive, inclusive, and intentional.

Originally published in June 2012. Reprint R1206D

Strategic Intent

by Gary Hamel and C.K. Prahalad

Editor's Note: When Gary Hamel, then a lecturer at London Business School, and C.K. Prahalad, a University of Michigan professor, first wrote "Strategic Intent," the article signaled that a major new force had arrived in management.

Hamel and Prahalad argue that Western companies focus on trimming their ambitions to match resources and, as a result, search only for advantages they can sustain. By contrast, Japanese corporations leverage resources by accelerating the pace of organizational learning and try to attain seemingly impossible goals. These firms foster the desire to succeed among their employees and maintain it by spreading the vision of global leadership. This is how Canon sought to "beat Xerox" and Komatsu set out to "encircle Caterpillar."

This strategic intent usually incorporates stretch targets, which force companies to compete in innovative ways. In this McKinsey Award–winning article, Hamel and Prahalad describe four techniques that Japanese companies use: building layers of advantage, searching for "loose bricks," changing the terms of engagement, and competing through collaboration.

TODAY MANAGERS IN MANY INDUSTRIES are working hard to match the competitive advantages of their new global rivals. They are moving manufacturing offshore in search of lower labor costs, rationalizing product lines to capture global scale economies, instituting quality circles and just-in-time production, and adopting Japanese human resource practices. When competitiveness still seems out of reach, they form strategic alliances—often with the very companies that upset the competitive balance in the first place.

Important as these initiatives are, few of them go beyond mere imitation. Too many companies are expending enormous energy simply to reproduce the cost and quality advantages their global competitors already enjoy. Imitation may be the sincerest form of flattery, but it will not lead to competitive revitalization. Strategies based on imitation are transparent to competitors who have already mastered them. Moreover, successful competitors rarely stand still. So it is not surprising that many executives feel trapped in a seemingly endless game of catch-up, regularly surprised by the new accomplishments of their rivals.

For these executives and their companies, regaining competitiveness will mean rethinking many of the basic concepts of strategy.[1] As "strategy" has blossomed, the competitiveness of Western companies has withered. This may be coincidence, but we think not. We believe that the application of concepts such as "strategic fit" (between resources and opportunities), "generic strategies" (low cost versus differentiation versus focus), and the "strategy hierarchy" (goals, strategies, and tactics) has often abetted the process of competitive decline. The new global competitors approach strategy from a perspective that is fundamentally different from that which underpins Western management thought. Against such competitors, marginal adjustments to current orthodoxies are no more likely to produce competitive revitalization than are marginal improvements in operating efficiency. (The sidebar "Remaking Strategy" describes our research and summarizes the two contrasting approaches to strategy we see in large multinational companies.)

Few Western companies have an enviable track record anticipating the moves of new global competitors. Why? The explanation begins with the way most companies have approached competitor analysis. Typically, competitor analysis focuses on the existing resources (human, technical, and financial) of present competitors. The only companies seen as a threat are those with the resources to erode margins and market share in the next planning period. Resourcefulness, the pace at which new competitive advantages are being built, rarely enters in.

Idea in Brief

If your company is struggling to outsmart formidable rivals, beware the flaws of traditional strategic planning approaches. They cause managers to misjudge the threat posed by more inventive and determined players, and prompt them to scale down their competitive aspirations to match current resources.

Managers who secure a leadership position for their company approach strategy from a very different angle. They nurture ambitions out of all proportion to their firm's current resources and capabilities. They fuel an obsessive will to win at every level of the organization—and sustain it over decades. And they define a long-term **strategic intent** that captures employees' imaginations and clarifies criteria for success—for example, Canon set out to "Beat Xerox." The payoff? Their companies take the lead and *keep* it—trapping also-rans in an endless game of catch-up.

In this respect, traditional competitor analysis is like a snapshot of a moving car. By itself, the photograph yields little information about the car's speed or direction—whether the driver is out for a quiet Sunday drive or warming up for the Grand Prix. Yet many managers have learned through painful experience that a business's initial resource endowment (whether bountiful or meager) is an unreliable predictor of future global success.

Think back: In 1970, few Japanese companies possessed the resource base, manufacturing volume, or technical prowess of U.S. and European industry leaders. Komatsu was less than 35% as large as Caterpillar (measured by sales), was scarcely represented outside Japan, and relied on just one product line—small bulldozers—for most of its revenue. Honda was smaller than American Motors and had not yet begun to export cars to the United States. Canon's first halting steps in the reprographics business looked pitifully small compared with the $4 billion Xerox powerhouse.

If Western managers had extended their competitor analysis to include these companies, it would merely have underlined how dramatic the resource discrepancies between them were. Yet by 1985, Komatsu was a $2.8 billion company with a product scope encompassing a broad range of earth-moving equipment, industrial

Idea in Practice

Turn Strategic Intent into Reality

Picture strategic intent as a marathon run in 400-meter sprints. You can't know what the terrain at mile 26 looks like, so you have to focus your company's attention on the next 400 meters. How? Present **corporate challenges**—each specifying the next hill in the race:

- **Create a sense of urgency.** Avoid future crises by exaggerating current indicators of potential threats. Heavy equipment manufacturer Komatsu budgeted based on worst-case exchange rates with an overvalued yen.

- **Personalize challenges.** When employees see exactly what best-in-class competitors are doing, they become personally focused on winning. Ford fired up workers with videos of Mazda's most efficient plant.

- **Give employees needed skills.** Provide training in statistical tools, problem solving, and team building.

- **Tackle one challenge at a time.** You'll avoid organizational overload and conflicting priorities.

Stay Ahead of Your Competition

With scarcer resources than your rivals', you need to continually outsmart your better-financed competition. Competitive innovation can help. Consider these approaches:

- **Build layers of advantages.** Don't rely on just one source of advantage, such as cheap

robots, and semiconductors. Honda manufactured almost as many cars worldwide in 1987 as Chrysler. Canon had matched Xerox's global unit market share.

The lesson is clear: Assessing the current tactical advantages of known competitors will not help you understand the resolution, stamina, or inventiveness of potential competitors. Sun-tzu, a Chinese military strategist, made the point 3,000 years ago: "All men can see the tactics whereby I conquer," he wrote, "but what none can see is the strategy out of which great victory is evolved."

Companies that have risen to global leadership over the past 20 years invariably began with ambitions that were out of all proportion to their resources and capabilities. But they created an obsession with winning at all levels of the organization and then labor. Also build your brand, increase your distribution channels, and tailor your products to unique markets.

- **Stake out undefended territory.** Honda identified "low end" motorcycles as an uncontested market. While selling 50cc bikes in the United States, it raced bigger ones in Europe—assembling the design skills and technology it needed to dominate the entire business. Rivals never saw Honda's strategic intent and growing competence in engines and power trains.

- **Change the terms of engagement.** While Xerox built a wide range of copiers it leased to corporate copy centers through a huge sales force, Canon standardized copy machines and components to reduce costs, sold its offerings outright through office-product dealers, and appealed to people who wanted their own machines. By developing capabilities that contrasted with Xerox's, Canon created a new "recipe" for success, short-circuiting Xerox's ability to retaliate quickly.

- **Compete through collaboration.** Electronics manufacturer Fujitsu's alliances with Siemens and British computer maker STC and with Amdahl in the United States boosted their manufacturing capacity and opened doors to Western markets.

sustained that obsession over the 10- to 20-year quest for global leadership. We term this obsession "strategic intent."

On the one hand, strategic intent envisions a desired leadership position and establishes the criterion the organization will use to chart its progress. Komatsu set out to "encircle Caterpillar." Canon sought to "beat Xerox." Honda strove to become a second Ford—an automotive pioneer. All are expressions of strategic intent.

At the same time, strategic intent is more than simply unfettered ambition. (Many companies possess an ambitious strategic intent yet fall short of their goals.) The concept also encompasses an active management process that includes focusing the organization's attention on the essence of winning, motivating people by communicating the value of the target, leaving room for individual and team

Remaking Strategy

OVER THE LAST TEN YEARS, our research on global competition, international alliances, and multinational management has brought us into close contact with senior managers in the United States, Europe, and Japan. As we tried to unravel the reasons for success and surrender in global markets, we became more and more suspicious that executives in Western and Far Eastern companies often operated with very different conceptions of competitive strategy. Understanding these differences, we thought, might help explain the conduct and outcome of competitive battles as well as supplement traditional explanations for Japan's ascendance and the West's decline.

We began by mapping the implicit strategy models of managers who had participated in our research. Then we built detailed histories of selected competitive battles. We searched for evidence of divergent views of strategy, competitive advantage, and the role of top management.

Two contrasting models of strategy emerged. One, which most Western managers will recognize, centers on the problem of maintaining strategic fit. The other centers on the problem of leveraging resources. The two are not mutually exclusive, but they represent a significant difference in emphasis—an emphasis that deeply affects how competitive battles get played out over time.

Both models recognize the problem of competing in a hostile environment with limited resources. But while the emphasis in the first is on trimming ambitions to match available resources, the emphasis in the second is on leveraging resources to reach seemingly unattainable goals.

Both models recognize that relative competitive advantage determines relative profitability. The first emphasizes the search for advantages that are inherently sustainable, the second emphasizes the need to accelerate organizational learning to outpace competitors in building new advantages.

Both models recognize the difficulty of competing against larger competitors. But while the first leads to a search for niches (or simply dissuades the

contributions, sustaining enthusiasm by providing new operational definitions as circumstances change, and using intent consistently to guide resource allocations.

Strategic intent captures the essence of winning

The Apollo program—landing a man on the moon ahead of the Soviets—was as competitively focused as Komatsu's drive against company from challenging an entrenched competitor), the second produces a quest for new rules that can devalue the incumbent's advantages.

Both models recognize that balance in the scope of an organization's activities reduces risk. The first seeks to reduce financial risk by building a balanced portfolio of cash-generating and cash-consuming businesses. The second seeks to reduce competitive risk by ensuring a well-balanced and sufficiently broad portfolio of advantages.

Both models recognize the need to disaggregate the organization in a way that allows top management to differentiate among the investment needs of various planning units. In the first model, resources are allocated to product-market units in which relatedness is defined by common products, channels, and customers. Each business is assumed to own all the critical skills it needs to execute its strategy successfully. In the second, investments are made in core competences (microprocessor controls or electronic imaging, for example) as well as in product-market units. By tracking these investments across businesses, top management works to assure that the plans of individual strategic units don't undermine future developments by default.

Both models recognize the need for consistency in action across organizational levels. In the first, consistency between corporate and business levels is largely a matter of conforming to financial objectives. Consistency between business and functional levels comes by tightly restricting the means the business uses to achieve its strategy—establishing standard operating procedures, defining the served market, adhering to accepted industry practices. In the second model, business-corporate consistency comes from allegiance to a particular strategic intent. Business-functional consistency comes from allegiance to intermediate-term goals or challenges with lower-level employees encouraged to invent how those goals will be achieved.

Caterpillar. The space program became the scorecard for America's technology race with the USSR. In the turbulent information technology industry, it was hard to pick a single competitor as a target, so NEC's strategic intent, set in the early 1970s, was to acquire the technologies that would put it in the best position to exploit the convergence of computing and telecommunications. Other industry observers foresaw this convergence, but only NEC made convergence

the guiding theme for subsequent strategic decisions by adopting "computing and communications" as its intent. For Coca-Cola,
strategic intent has been to put a Coke within "arm's reach" of every
consumer in the world.

Strategic intent is stable over time
In battles for global leadership, one of the most critical tasks is to
lengthen the organization's attention span. Strategic intent provides
consistency to short-term action, while leaving room for reinterpre-
tation as new opportunities emerge. At Komatsu, encircling Caterpillar encompassed a succession of medium-term programs aimed
at exploiting specific weaknesses in Caterpillar or building particular
competitive advantages. When Caterpillar threatened Komatsu in
Japan, for example, Komatsu responded by first improving quality,
then driving down costs, then cultivating export markets, and then
underwriting new product development.

Strategic intent sets a target that deserves personal effort and commitment
Ask the CEOs of many American corporations how they measure
their contributions to their companies' success, and you're likely to
get an answer expressed in terms of shareholder wealth. In a company that possesses a strategic intent, top management is more likely
to talk in terms of global market leadership. Market share leadership
typically yields shareholder wealth, to be sure. But the two goals do
not have the same motivational impact. It is hard to imagine middle
managers, let alone blue-collar employees, waking up each day with
the sole thought of creating more shareholder wealth. But mightn't
they feel different given the challenge to "beat Benz"—the rallying
cry at one Japanese auto producer? Strategic intent gives employees
the only goal that is worthy of commitment: to unseat the best or
remain the best, worldwide.

Many companies are more familiar with strategic planning than
they are with strategic intent. The planning process typically acts
as a "feasibility sieve." Strategies are accepted or rejected on the
basis of whether managers can be precise about the "how" as well

as the "what" of their plans. Are the milestones clear? Do we have the necessary skills and resources? How will competitors react? Has the market been thoroughly researched? In one form or another, the admonition "Be realistic!" is given to line managers at almost every turn.

But can you *plan* for global leadership? Did Komatsu, Canon, and Honda have detailed, 20-year strategies for attacking Western markets? Are Japanese and Korean managers better planners than their Western counterparts? No. As valuable as strategic planning is, global leadership is an objective that lies outside the range of planning. We know of few companies with highly developed planning systems that have managed to set a strategic intent. As tests of strategic fit become more stringent, goals that cannot be planned for fall by the wayside. Yet companies that are afraid to commit to goals that lie outside the range of planning are unlikely to become global leaders.

Although strategic planning is billed as a way of becoming more future oriented, most managers, when pressed, will admit that their strategic plans reveal more about today's problems than tomorrow's opportunities. With a fresh set of problems confronting managers at the beginning of every planning cycle, focus often shifts dramatically from year to year. And with the pace of change accelerating in most industries, the predictive horizon is becoming shorter and shorter. So plans do little more than project the present forward incrementally. The goal of strategic intent is to fold the future back into the present. The important question is not "How will next year be different from this year?" but "What must we do differently next year to get closer to our strategic intent?" Only with a carefully articulated and adhered to strategic intent will a succession of year-on-year plans sum up to global leadership.

Just as you cannot plan a ten- to 20-year quest for global leadership, the chance of falling into a leadership position by accident is also remote. We don't believe that global leadership comes from an undirected process of intrapreneurship. Nor is it the product of a Skunk Works or other technique for internal venturing. Behind such programs lies a nihilistic assumption: that the organization is so hidebound, so orthodox ridden, the only way to innovate is to put a few bright people in a dark room, pour in some money, and hope that something wonderful will happen. In this Silicon Valley approach to innovation, the only role for top managers is to retrofit their corporate strategy to the entrepreneurial successes that emerge from below. Here the value added of top management is low indeed.

Sadly, this view of innovation may be consistent with reality in many large companies.[2] On the one hand, top management lacks any particular point of view about desirable ends beyond satisfying shareholders and keeping raiders at bay. On the other, the planning format, reward criteria, definition of served market, and belief in accepted industry practice all work together to tightly constrain the range of available means. As a result, innovation is necessarily an isolated activity. Growth depends more on the inventive capacity of individuals and small teams than on the ability of top management to aggregate the efforts of multiple teams toward an ambitious strategic intent.

In companies that have overcome resource constraints to build leadership positions, we see a different relationship between means and ends. While strategic intent is clear about ends, it is flexible as to means—it leaves room for improvisation. Achieving strategic intent requires enormous creativity with respect to means: Witness Fujitsu's use of strategic alliances in Europe to attack IBM. But this creativity comes in the service of a clearly prescribed end. Creativity is unbridled but not uncorralled, because top management establishes the criterion against which employees can pretest the logic of their initiatives. Middle managers must do more than deliver on promised financial targets; they must also deliver on the broad direction implicit in their organization's strategic intent.

Strategic intent implies a sizable stretch for an organization. Current capabilities and resources will not suffice. This forces the organization to be more inventive, to make the most of limited resources. Whereas the traditional view of strategy focuses on the degree of fit between existing resources and current opportunities, strategic intent creates an extreme misfit between resources and ambitions. Top management then challenges the organization to close the gap by systematically building new advantages. For Canon, this meant first understanding Xerox's patents, then licensing technology to create a product that would yield early market experience, then gearing up internal R&D efforts, then licensing its own technology to other manufacturers to fund further R&D, then entering market segments in Japan and Europe where Xerox was weak, and so on.

In this respect, strategic intent is like a marathon run in 400-meter sprints. No one knows what the terrain will look like at mile 26, so the role of top management is to focus the organization's attention on the ground to be covered in the next 400 meters. In several companies, management did this by presenting the organization with a series of corporate challenges, each specifying the next hill in the race to achieve strategic intent. One year the challenge might be quality, the next it might be total customer care, the next, entry into new markets, and the next, a rejuvenated product line. As this example indicates, corporate challenges are a way to stage the acquisition of new competitive advantages, a way to identify the focal point for employees' efforts in the near to medium term. As with strategic intent, top management is specific about the ends (reducing product development times by 75%, for example) but less prescriptive about the means.

Like strategic intent, challenges stretch the organization. To preempt Xerox in the personal copier business, Canon set its engineers a target price of $1,000 for a home copier. At the time, Canon's least expensive copier sold for several thousand dollars. Trying to reduce the cost of existing models would not have given Canon the radical price-performance improvement it needed to delay or deter Xerox's entry into personal copiers. Instead, Canon engineers were challenged to reinvent the copier—a challenge they met by substituting a disposable cartridge for the complex image-transfer mechanism used in other copiers.

Corporate challenges come from analyzing competitors as well as from the foreseeable pattern of industry evolution. Together these reveal potential competitive openings and identify the new skills the organization will need to take the initiative away from better-positioned players. (The exhibit "Building competitive advantage at Komatsu" illustrates the way challenges helped Komatsu achieve its intent.)

97

Building competitive advantage at Komatsu

Corporate challenge	Protect Komatsu's home market against Caterpillar		Reduce costs while maintaining quality	
Programs	early 1960s	Licensing deals with Cummins Engine, International Harvester, and Bucyrus-Erie to acquire technology and establish benchmarks	1965	Cost Down (CD) program
	1961	Project A (for Ace) to advance the product quality of Komatsu's small and midsize bull-dozers above Caterpillar's	1966	Total CD program
	1962	Quality circles company-wide to provide training for all employees		

Make Komatsu an international enterprise and build export markets		Respond to external shocks that threaten markets		Create new products and markets	
early 1960s	Develop Eastern bloc countries	1975	V-10 program to reduce costs by 10% while maintaining quality; reduce parts by 20%; rationalize manufacturing system	late 1970s	Accelerate product development to expand line
1967	Komatsu Europe marketing subsidiary established	1977	¥180 program to budget companywide for 180 yen to the dollar when exchange rate was 240	1979	Future and Frontiers program to identify new businesses based on society's needs and company's know-how
1970	Komatsu America established	1979	Project E to establish teams to redouble cost and quality efforts in response to oil crisis	1981	EPOCHS program to reconcile greater product variety with improved production efficiencies
1972	Project B to improve the durability and reliability and to reduce costs of large bulldozers				
1972	Project C to improve payloaders				
1972	Project D to improve hydraulic excavators				
1974	Establish presales and service departments to assist newly industrializing countries in construction projects				

For a challenge to be effective, individuals and teams through-out the organization must understand it and see its implications for their own jobs. Companies that set corporate challenges to cre-ate new competitive advantages (as Ford and IBM did with quality improvement) quickly discover that engaging the entire organiza-tion requires top management to do the following:

- *Create a sense of urgency,* or quasi crisis, by amplifying weak signals in the environment that point up the need to improve, instead of allowing inaction to precipitate a real crisis. Komatsu, for example, budgeted on the basis of worst-case exchange rates that overvalued the yen.

- *Develop a competitor focus at every level through widespread use of competitive intelligence.* Every employee should be able to benchmark his or her efforts against best-in-class compet-itors so that the challenge becomes personal. For instance, Ford showed production-line workers videotapes of opera-tions at Mazda's most efficient plant.

- *Provide employees with the skills they need to work effectively—* training in statistical tools, problem solving, value engineer-ing, and team building, for example.

- *Give the organization time to digest one challenge before launching another.* When competing initiatives overload the organization, middle managers often try to protect their people from the whipsaw of shifting priorities. But this "wait and see if they're serious this time" attitude ultimately destroys the credibility of corporate challenges.

- *Establish clear milestones and review mechanisms* to track progress, and ensure that internal recognition and rewards reinforce desired behaviors. The goal is to make the challenge inescapable for everyone in the company.

It is important to distinguish between the process of man-aging corporate challenges and the advantages that the process creates. Whatever the actual challenge may be—quality, cost, value engineering, or something else—there is the same need to engage employees intellectually and emotionally in the development of new skills. In each case, the challenge will take root only if senior executives and lower-level employees feel a reciprocal responsibility for competitiveness.

We believe workers in many companies have been asked to take a disproportionate share of the blame for competitive failure. In one U.S. company, for example, management had sought a 40% wage-package concession from hourly employees to bring labor costs into line with Far Eastern competitors. The result was a long strike and, ultimately, a 10% wage concession from employees on the line. However, direct labor costs in manufacturing accounted for less than 15% of total value added. The company thus succeeded in demoralizing its entire blue-collar workforce for the sake of a 1.5% reduction in total costs. Ironically, further analysis showed that their competitors' most significant costs savings came not from lower hourly wages but from better work methods invented by employees. You can imagine how eager the U.S. workers were to make similar contributions after the strike and concessions. Contrast this situation with what happened at Nissan when the yen strengthened: Top management took a big pay cut and then asked middle managers and line employees to sacrifice relatively less.

Reciprocal responsibility means shared gain and shared pain. In too many companies, the pain of revitalization falls almost exclusively on the employees least responsible for the enterprise's decline. Too often, workers are asked to commit to corporate goals without any matching commitment from top management—be it employment security, gain sharing, or an ability to influence the direction of the business. This one-sided approach to regaining competitiveness keeps many companies from harnessing the intellectual horsepower of their employees.

Creating a sense of reciprocal responsibility is crucial because competitiveness ultimately depends on the pace at which a company embeds new advantages deep within its organization, not on its stock of advantages at any given time. Thus, the concept of competitive advantage must be expanded beyond the scorecard many managers now use: Are my costs lower? Will my product command a price premium?

Few competitive advantages are long lasting. Uncovering a new competitive advantage is a bit like getting a hot tip on a stock: The first person to act on the insight makes more money than the last. When the experience curve was young, a company that built capacity ahead of competitors, dropped prices to fill plants, and reduced costs as volume rose went to the bank. The first mover traded on the fact that competitors undervalued market share—they didn't price to capture additional share because they didn't understand how market share leadership could be translated into lower costs and better margins. But there is no more undervalued market share when each of 20 semiconductor companies builds enough capacity to serve 10% of the world market.

Keeping score of existing advantages is not the same as building new advantages. The essence of strategy lies in creating tomorrow's competitive advantages faster than competitors mimic the ones you possess today. In the 1960s, Japanese producers relied on labor and capital cost advantages. As Western manufacturers began to move production offshore, Japanese companies accelerated their investment in process technology and created scale and quality advantages. Then, as their U.S. and European competitors rationalized manufacturing, they added another string to their bow by accelerating the rate of product development. Then they built global brands. Then they deskilled competitors through alliances and outsourcing deals. The moral? An organization's capacity to improve existing skills and learn new ones is the most defensible competitive advantage of all.

To achieve a strategic intent, a company must usually take on larger, better-financed competitors. That means carefully managing competitive engagements so that scarce resources are conserved. Managers cannot do that simply by playing the same game better—making marginal improvements to competitors' technology and business practices. Instead, they must fundamentally change the game in ways that disadvantage incumbents: devising novel approaches to market entry, advantage building, and competitive warfare. For smart competitors, the goal is not competitive imitation but competitive innovation, the art of containing competitive risks within manageable proportions.

Four approaches to competitive innovation are evident in the global expansion of Japanese companies. These are: building layers of advantage, searching for loose bricks, changing the terms of engagement, and competing through collaboration.

The wider a company's portfolio of advantages, the less risk it faces in competitive battles. New global competitors have built such portfolios by steadily expanding their arsenals of competitive weapons. They have moved inexorably from less defensible advantages such as low wage costs to more defensible advantages such as global brands. The Japanese color television industry illustrates this layering process.

By 1967, Japan had become the largest producer of black-and-white television sets. By 1970, it was closing the gap in color televisions. Japanese manufacturers used their competitive advantage—at that time, primarily, low labor costs—to build a base in the private-label business, then moved quickly to establish world-scale plants. This investment gave them additional layers of advantage—quality and reliability—as well as further cost reductions from process improvements. At the same time, they recognized that these cost-based advantages were vulnerable to changes in labor costs, process and product technology, exchange rates, and trade policy. So throughout the 1970s, they also invested heavily in building channels and brands, thus creating another layer of advantage: a global franchise. In the late 1970s, they enlarged the scope of their products and businesses to amortize these grand investments, and by 1980 all the major players—Matsushita, Sharp, Toshiba, Hitachi, Sanyo—had established related sets of businesses that could support global marketing investments. More recently, they have been investing in regional manufacturing and design centers to tailor their products more closely to national markets.

These manufacturers thought of the various sources of competitive advantage as mutually desirable layers, not mutually exclusive choices. What some call competitive suicide—pursuing both cost and differentiation—is exactly what many competitors strive for.[3] Using flexible manufacturing technologies and better marketing intelligence, they are moving away from standardized "world products" to products like Mazda's minivan, developed in California expressly for the U.S. market.

Another approach to competitive innovation, searching for loose bricks, exploits the benefits of surprise, which is just as useful in business battles as it is in war. Particularly in the early stages of a war for global markets, successful new competitors work to stay below the response threshold of their larger, more powerful rivals. Staking out underdefended territory is one way to do this.

To find loose bricks, managers must have few orthodoxies about how to break into a market or challenge a competitor. For example, in one large U.S. multinational, we asked several country managers to describe what a Japanese competitor was doing in the local market. The first executive said, "They're coming at us in the low end. Japanese companies always come in at the bottom." The second speaker found the comment interesting but disagreed: "They don't offer any low-end products in my market, but they have some exciting stuff at the top end. We really should reverse engineer that thing." Another colleague told still another story. "They haven't taken any business away from me," he said, "but they've just made me a great offer to supply components." In each country, the Japanese competitor had found a different loose brick.

The search for loose bricks begins with a careful analysis of the competitor's conventional wisdom: How does the company define its "served market"? What activities are most profitable? Which geographic markets are too troublesome to enter? The objective is not to find a corner of the industry (or niche) where larger competitors seldom tread but to build a base of attack just outside the market territory that industry leaders currently occupy. The goal is an uncontested profit sanctuary, which could be a particular product segment (the "low end" in motorcycles), a slice of the value chain (components in the computer industry), or a particular geographic market (Eastern Europe).

When Honda took on leaders in the motorcycle industry, for example, it began with products that were just outside the conventional definition of the leaders' product-market domains. As a result, it could build a base of operations in underdefended territory and then use that base to launch an expanded attack. What many competitors failed to see was Honda's strategic intent and its growing competence in engines and power trains. Yet even as Honda was selling 50cc motorcycles in the United States, it was already racing larger bikes in Europe—assembling the design skills and technology it would need for a systematic expansion across the entire spectrum of motor-related businesses.

Honda's progress in creating a core competence in engines should have warned competitors that it might enter a series of seemingly unrelated industries—automobiles, lawn mowers, marine engines, generators. But with each company fixated on its own market, the threat of Honda's horizontal diversification went unnoticed. Today, companies like Matsushita and Toshiba are similarly poised to move in unexpected ways across industry boundaries. In protecting loose bricks, companies must extend their peripheral vision by tracking and anticipating the migration of global competitors across product segments, businesses, national markets, value-added stages, and distribution channels.

Changing the terms of engagement—refusing to accept the front-runner's definition of industry and segment boundaries—represents still another form of competitive innovation. Canon's entry into the copier business illustrates this approach.

During the 1970s, both Kodak and IBM tried to match Xerox's business system in terms of segmentation, products, distribution, service, and pricing. As a result, Xerox had no trouble decoding the new entrants' intentions and developing countermoves. IBM eventually withdrew from the copier business, while Kodak remains a distant second in the large copier market that Xerox still dominates.

Canon, on the other hand, changed the terms of competitive engagement. While Xerox built a wide range of copiers, Canon standardized machines and components to reduce costs. It chose to distribute through office product dealers rather than try to match

Xerox's huge direct sales force. It also avoided the need to create a national service network by designing reliability and serviceability into its product and then delegating service responsibility to the dealers. Canon copiers were sold rather than leased, freeing Canon from the burden of financing the lease base. Finally, instead of selling to the heads of corporate duplicating departments, Canon appealed to secretaries and department managers who wanted distributed copying. At each stage, Canon neatly sidestepped a potential barrier to entry.

Canon's experience suggests that there is an important distinction between barriers to entry and barriers to imitation. Competitors that tried to match Xerox's business system had to pay the same entry costs—the barriers to imitation were high. But Canon dramatically reduced the barriers to entry by changing the rules of the game.

Changing the rules also short-circuited Xerox's ability to retaliate quickly against its new rival. Confronted with the need to rethink its business strategy and organization, Xerox was paralyzed for a time. Its managers realized that the faster they downsized the product line, developed new channels, and improved reliability, the faster they would erode the company's traditional profit base. What might have been seen as critical success factors—Xerox's national sales force and service network, its large installed base of leased machines, and its reliance on service revenues—instead became barriers to retaliation. In this sense, competitive innovation is like judo: The goal is to use a larger competitor's weight against it. And that happens not by matching the leader's capabilities but by developing contrasting capabilities of one's own.

Competitive innovation works on the premise that a successful competitor is likely to be wedded to a recipe for success. That's why the most effective weapon new competitors possess is probably a clean sheet of paper. And why an incumbent's greatest vulnerability is its belief in accepted practice.

Through licensing, outsourcing agreements, and joint ventures, it is sometimes possible to win without fighting. For example, Fujitsu's alliances in Europe with Siemens and STC (Britain's largest computer maker) and in the United States with Amdahl yield manufacturing volume and access to Western markets. In the early 1980s, Matsushita established a joint venture with Thorn (in the United Kingdom), Telefunken (in Germany), and Thomson (in France), which allowed it to quickly multiply the forces arrayed against Philips in the battle for leadership in the European VCR business. In fighting larger global rivals by proxy, Japanese companies have adopted a maxim as old as human conflict itself: My enemy's enemy is my friend.

Hijacking the development efforts of potential rivals is another goal of competitive collaboration. In the consumer electronics war, Japanese competitors attacked traditional businesses like TVs and hi-fis while volunteering to manufacture next generation products like VCRs, camcorders, and CD players for Western rivals. They hoped their rivals would ratchet down development spending, and, in most cases, that is precisely what happened. But companies that abandoned their own development efforts seldom reemerged as serious competitors in subsequent new product battles.

Collaboration can also be used to calibrate competitors' strengths and weaknesses. Toyota's joint venture with GM, and Mazda's with Ford, give these automakers an invaluable vantage point for assessing the progress their U.S. rivals have made in cost reduction, quality, and technology. They can also learn how GM and Ford compete— when they will fight and when they won't. Of course, the reverse is also true: Ford and GM have an equal opportunity to learn from their partner-competitors.

The route to competitive revitalization we have been mapping implies a new view of strategy. Strategic intent assures consistency in resource allocation over the long term. Clearly articulated corporate challenges focus the efforts of individuals in the medium term. Finally, competitive innovation helps reduce competitive risk in the short term. This consistency in the long term, focus in the medium term, and inventiveness and involvement in the short term provide the key to leveraging limited resources in pursuit of ambitious goals. But just as there is a process of winning, so there is a process of surrender. Revitalization requires understanding that process, too.

The Process of Surrender

ON THE BATTLES FOR GLOBAL LEADERSHIP that have taken place during the past two decades, we have seen a pattern of competitive attack and retrenchment that was remarkably similar across industries. We call this the process of surrender.

The process started with unseen intent. Not possessing long-term, competitor-focused goals themselves, Western companies did not ascribe such intentions to their rivals. They also calculated the threat posed by potential competitors in terms of their existing resources rather than their resourcefulness. This led to systematic underestimation of smaller rivals who were fast gaining technology through licensing arrangements, acquiring market understanding from downstream OEM partners, and improving product quality and manufacturing productivity through company-wide employee involvement programs. Oblivious of the strategic intent and intangible advantages of their rivals, American and European businesses were caught off guard.

Adding to the competitive surprise was the fact that the new entrants typically attacked the periphery of a market (Honda in small motorcycles, Yamaha in grand pianos, Toshiba in small black-and-white televisions) before going head-to-head with incumbents. Incumbents often misread these attacks, seeing them as part of a niche strategy and not as a search for "loose bricks." Unconventional market entry strategies (minority holdings in less-developed countries, use of nontraditional channels, extensive corporate advertising) were ignored or dismissed as quirky. For example, managers we spoke with said Japanese companies' position in the European computer industry was nonexistent. In terms of brand share that's nearly true, but the Japanese control as much as one-third of the manufacturing value added in the hardware sales of European-based computer businesses. Similarly, German auto producers claimed to feel unconcerned over the proclivity of Japanese producers to move upmarket. But with its low-end models under tremendous pressure from Japanese producers, Porsche has now announced that it will no longer make "entry level" cars.

Western managers often misinterpreted their rivals' tactics. They believed that Japanese and Korean companies were competing solely on the basis of cost and quality. This typically produced a partial response to those competitors'

Given their technological leadership and access to large regional markets, how did U.S. and European countries lose their apparent birthright to dominate global industries? There is no simple answer. Few companies recognize the value of documenting failure. Fewer still search their own managerial orthodoxies for the seeds of competitive

```
┌──────────────┐   ┌──────────────┐   ┌──────────────┐
│   Unseen     │   │ Underestimated│   │Unconventional│
│strategic intent│ │resourcefulness│  │entry tactics │
└──────────────┘   └──────────────┘   └──────────────┘
                          │
                          ▼
                   ┌──────────────┐
                   │ Competitive  │
                   │  surprise    │
                   └──────────────┘
                          │
                          ▼
                   ┌──────────────┐
                   │   Partial    │
                   │  response    │
                   └──────────────┘
                          │
                          ▼
                   ┌──────────────┐
                   │  Catch-up    │
                   │    trap      │
                   └──────────────┘
                          │
                          ▼
                   ┌──────────────┐
                   │    Lost      │
                   │   battles    │
                   └──────────────┘
                          │
                          ▼
                   ┌──────────────┐
                   │   Sense of   │
                   │ inevitability│
                   └──────────────┘
                          │
                          ▼
                   ┌──────────────┐
                   │   Retreat    │
                   │   and exit   │
                   └──────────────┘
```

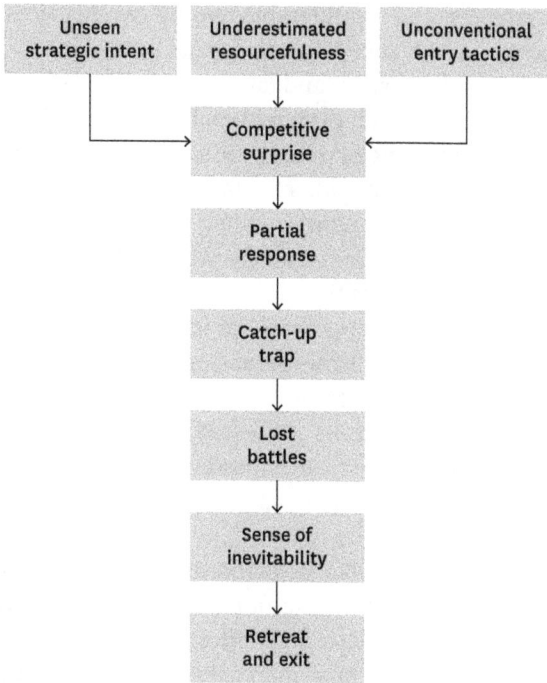

initiatives: moving manufacturing offshore, outsourcing, or instituting a quality program. Seldom was the full extent of the competitive threat appreciated—the multiple layers of advantage, the expansion across related product segments, the development of global brand positions. Imitating the currently visible tactics of rivals put Western businesses into a perpetual catch-up trap. One by one, companies lost battles and came to see surrender as inevitable. Surrender was not inevitable, of course, but the attack was staged in a way that disguised ultimate intentions and sidestepped direct confrontation.

surrender. But we believe there is a pathology of surrender that gives some important clues. (See the sidebar "The Process of Surrender.")

It is not very comforting to think that the essence of Western strategic thought can be reduced to eight rules for excellence, seven S's, five competitive forces, four product life-cycle stages, three generic strategies, and innumerable two-by-two matrices.[4] Yet for the past 20 years, "advances" in strategy have taken the form of ever more typologies, heuristics, and laundry lists, often with dubious empirical bases. Moreover, even reasonable concepts like the product life cycle, experience curve, product portfolios, and generic strategies often have toxic side effects: They reduce the number of strategic options management is willing to consider. They create a preference for selling businesses rather than defending them. They yield predictable strategies that rivals easily decode.

Strategy recipes limit opportunities for competitive innovation. A company may have 40 businesses and only four strategies—invest, hold, harvest, or divest. Too often, strategy is seen as a positioning exercise in which options are tested by how they fit the existing industry structure. But current industry structure reflects the strengths of the industry leader, and playing by the leader's rules is usually competitive suicide.

Armed with concepts like segmentation, the value chain, competitor benchmarking, strategic groups, and mobility barriers, many managers have become better and better at drawing industry maps. But while they have been busy mapmaking, their competitors have been moving entire continents. The strategist's goal is not to find a niche within the existing industry space but to create new space that is uniquely suited to the company's own strengths—space that is off the map.

This is particularly true now that industry boundaries are becoming more and more unstable. In industries such as financial services and communications, rapidly changing technology, deregulation, and globalization have undermined the value of traditional industry analysis. Mapmaking skills are worth little in the epicenter of an earthquake. But an industry in upheaval presents opportunities for ambitious companies to redraw the map in their favor, so long as they can think outside traditional industry boundaries.

Concepts like "mature" and "declining" are largely definitional. What most executives mean when they label a business "mature" is that sales growth has stagnated in their current geographic markets for existing products sold through existing channels. In such cases, it's not the industry that is mature, but the executives' conception of the industry. Asked if the piano business was mature, a senior executive at Yamaha replied, "Only if we can't take any market share from anybody anywhere in the world and still make money. And anyway, we're not in the 'piano' business, we're in the 'keyboard' business." Year after year, Sony has revitalized its radio and tape recorder businesses, despite the fact that other manufacturers long ago abandoned these businesses as mature.

A narrow concept of maturity can foreclose a company from a broad stream of future opportunities. In the 1970s, several U.S. companies thought that consumer electronics had become a mature industry. What could possibly top the color TV? they asked themselves. RCA and GE, distracted by opportunities in more "attractive" industries like mainframe computers, left Japanese producers with a virtual monopoly in VCRs, camcorders, and CD players. Ironically, the TV business, once thought mature, is on the verge of a dramatic renaissance. A $20 billion-a-year business will be created when high-definition television is launched in the United States. But the pioneers of television may capture only a small part of this bonanza.

Most of the tools of strategic analysis are focused domestically. Few force managers to consider global opportunities and threats. For example, portfolio planning portrays top management's investment options as an array of businesses rather than as an array of geographic markets. The result is predictable: As businesses come under attack from foreign competitors, the company attempts to abandon them and enter other areas in which the forces of global competition are not yet so strong. In the short term, this may be an appropriate response to waning competitiveness, but there are fewer and fewer businesses in which a domestic-oriented company can find refuge. We seldom hear such companies asking, Can we move into emerging markets overseas ahead of our global rivals and prolong the profitability of this business? Can we counterattack in our global competitors' home market and slow the pace of their expansion? A senior executive in one successful global company made a telling comment: "We're glad to find a competitor managing by the portfolio concept—we can almost predict how much share we'll have to take away to put the business on the CEO's 'sell list.' "

Companies can also be overcommitted to organizational recipes, such as strategic business units (SBUs) and the decentralization an SBU structure implies. Decentralization is seductive because it places the responsibility for success or failure squarely on the shoulders of line managers. Each business is assumed to have all the resources it needs to execute its strategies successfully, and in this no-excuses environment, it is hard for top management to fail. But desirable as clear lines of responsibility and accountability are, competitive revitalization requires positive value added from top management.

Few companies with a strong SBU orientation have built successful global distribution and brand positions. Investments in a global brand franchise typically transcend the resources and risk propensity of a single business. While some Western companies have had global brand positions for 30 or 40 years or more (Heinz, Siemens, IBM, Ford, and Kodak, for example), it is hard to identify any American or European company that has created a new global brand franchise in the past ten to 15 years. Yet Japanese companies have created a score or more—NEC, Fujitsu, Panasonic (Matsushita), Toshiba, Sony, Seiko, Epson, Canon, Minolta, and Honda among them.

General Electric's situation is typical. In many of its businesses, this American giant has been almost unknown in Europe and Asia. GE made no coordinated effort to build a global corporate franchise. Any GE business with international ambitions had to bear the burden of establishing its credibility and credentials in the new market alone. Not surprisingly, some once-strong GE businesses opted out of the difficult task of building a global brand position. By contrast, smaller Korean companies like Samsung, Daewoo, and Lucky-Goldstar are busy building global-brand umbrellas that will ease market entry for a whole range of businesses. The underlying principle is simple: Economies of scope may be as important as economies of scale in entering global markets. But capturing economies of scope demands interbusiness coordination that only top management can provide.

We believe that inflexible SBU-type organizations have also contributed to the de-skilling of some companies. For a single SBU, incapable of sustaining an investment in a core competence such as semiconductors, optical media, or combustion engines, the only way to remain competitive is to purchase key components from potential (often Japanese or Korean) competitors. For an SBU defined in product market terms, competitiveness means offering an end product that is competitive in price and performance. But that gives an SBU manager little incentive to distinguish between external sourcing that achieves "product embodied" competitiveness and internal development that yields deeply embedded organizational competencies that can be exploited across multiple businesses. Where upstream component-manufacturing activities are seen as cost centers with cost-plus transfer pricing, additional investment in the core activity may seem a less profitable use of capital than investment in downstream activities. To make matters worse, internal accounting data may not reflect the competitive value of retaining control over a core competence.

Together, a shared global corporate brand franchise and a shared core competence act as mortar in many Japanese companies. Lacking this mortar, a company's businesses are truly loose bricks—easily knocked out by global competitors that steadily invest in core competences. Such competitors can co-opt domestically oriented companies into long-term sourcing dependence and capture the economies of scope of global brand investment through interbusiness coordination.

Last in decentralization's list of dangers is the standard of managerial performance typically used in SBU organizations. In many companies, business unit managers are rewarded solely on the basis of their performance against return on investment targets. Unfortunately, that often leads to denominator management because executives soon discover that reductions in investment and head count—the denominator—"improve" the financial ratios by which they are measured more easily than growth in the numerator: revenues. It also fosters a hair-trigger sensitivity to industry down-turns that can be very costly. Managers who are quick to reduce investment and dismiss workers find it takes much longer to regain lost skills and catch up on investment when the industry turns upward again. As a result, they lose market share in every business cycle. Particularly in industries where there is fierce competition for the best people and where competitors invest relentlessly, denominator management creates a retrenchment ratchet.

The concept of the general manager as a movable peg reinforces the problem of denominator management. Business schools are guilty here because they have perpetuated the notion that a manager with net present value calculations in one hand and portfolio planning in the other can manage any business anywhere.

In many diversified companies, top management evaluates line managers on numbers alone because no other basis for dialogue exists. Managers move so many times as part of their "career development" that they often do not understand the nuances of the businesses they are managing. At GE, for example, one fast-track manager heading an important new venture had moved across five businesses in five years. His series of quick successes finally came to an end when he confronted a Japanese competitor whose managers had been plodding along in the same business for more than a decade.

Regardless of ability and effort, fast-track managers are unlikely to develop the deep business knowledge they need to discuss technology options, competitors' strategies, and global opportunities substantively. Invariably, therefore, discussions gravitate to "the numbers," while the value added of managers is limited to the financial and planning savvy they carry from job to job. Knowledge of the company's internal planning and accounting systems substitutes for substantive knowledge of the business, making competitive innovation unlikely.

When managers know that their assignments have a two- to three-year time frame, they feel great pressure to create a good track record fast. This pressure often takes one of two forms. Either the manager does not commit to goals whose time line extends beyond his or her expected tenure. Or ambitious goals are adopted and squeezed into an unrealistically short time frame. Aiming to be number one in a business is the essence of strategic intent; but imposing a three- to four-year horizon on the effort simply invites disaster. Acquisitions are made with little attention to the problems of integration. The organization becomes overloaded with initiatives. Collaborative ventures are formed without adequate attention to competitive consequences.

Almost every strategic management theory and nearly every corporate planning system is premised on a strategy hierarchy in which corporate goals guide business unit strategies and business unit strategies guide functional tactics.[5] In this hierarchy, senior management makes strategy and lower levels execute it. The dichotomy between formulation and implementation is familiar and widely accepted. But the strategy hierarchy undermines competitiveness by fostering an elitist view of management that tends to disenfranchise most of the organization. Employees fail to identify with corporate goals or involve themselves deeply in the work of becoming more competitive.

The strategy hierarchy isn't the only explanation for an elitist view of management, of course. The myths that grow up around successful top managers—"Lee Iacocca saved Chrysler," "Carlo De Benedetti rescued Olivetti," "John Sculley turned Apple around"— perpetuate it. So does the turbulent business environment. Middle managers buffeted by circumstances that seem to be beyond their control desperately want to believe that top management has all the answers. And top management, in turn, hesitates to admit it does not for fear of demoralizing lower-level employees.

The result of all this is often a code of silence in which the full extent of a company's competitiveness problem is not widely shared. We interviewed business unit managers in one company, for example, who were extremely anxious because top management wasn't talking openly about the competitive challenges the company faced. They assumed the lack of communication indicated a lack of awareness on their senior managers' part. But when asked whether they were open with their own employees, these same managers replied that while they could face up to the problems, the people below them could not. Indeed, the only time the workforce heard about the company's competitiveness problems was during wage negotiations when problems were used to extract concessions.

Unfortunately, a threat that everyone perceives but no one talks about creates more anxiety than a threat that has been clearly identified and made the focal point for the problem-solving efforts of the entire company. That is one reason honesty and humility on the part of top management may be the first prerequisite of revitalization. Another reason is the need to make "participation" more than a buzzword.

Programs such as quality circles and total customer service often fall short of expectations because management does not recognize that successful implementation requires more than administrative structures. Difficulties in embedding new capabilities are typically put down to "communication" problems, with the unstated assumption that if only downward communication were more effective—"if only middle management would get the message straight"—the new program would quickly take root. The need for upward communication is often ignored, or assumed to mean nothing more than feedback. In contrast, Japanese companies win not because they have smarter managers but because they have developed ways to harness the "wisdom of the anthill." They realize that top managers are a bit like the astronauts who circle the Earth in the space shuttle. It may be the astronauts who get all the glory, but everyone knows that the real intelligence behind the mission is located firmly on the ground.

Where strategy formulation is an elitist activity, it is also difficult to produce truly creative strategies. For one thing, there are not enough heads and points of view in divisional or corporate planning departments to challenge conventional wisdom. For another, creative strategies seldom emerge from the annual planning ritual. The starting point for next year's strategy is almost always this year's strategy. Improvements are incremental. The company sticks to the segments and territories it knows, even though the real opportunities may be elsewhere. The impetus for Canon's pioneering entry into the personal copier business came from an overseas sales subsidiary—not from planners in Japan.

The goal of the strategy hierarchy remains valid—to ensure consistency up and down the organization. But this consistency is better derived from a clearly articulated strategic intent than from inflexibly applied top-down plans. In the 1990s, the challenge will be to enfranchise employees to invent the means to accomplish ambitious ends.

We seldom found cautious administrators among the top managements of companies that came from behind to challenge incumbents for global leadership. But in studying organizations that had surrendered, we invariably found senior managers who, for whatever reason, lacked the courage to commit their companies to heroic goals—goals that lay beyond the reach of planning and existing resources. The conservative goals they set failed to generate pressure and enthusiasm for competitive innovation or give the organization much useful guidance. Financial targets and vague mission statements just cannot provide the consistent direction that is a prerequisite for winning a global competitive war.

This kind of conservatism is usually blamed on the financial markets. But we believe that in most cases, investors' so-called short-term orientation simply reflects a lack of confidence in the ability of senior managers to conceive and deliver stretch goals. The chairman of one company complained bitterly that even after improving return on capital employed to over 40% (by ruthlessly divesting lackluster businesses and downsizing others), the stock market held the company to an 8:1 price/earnings ratio. Of course, the market's message was clear: "We don't trust you. You've shown no ability to achieve profitable growth. Just cut out the slack, manage the denominators, and perhaps you'll be taken over by a company that can use your resources more creatively." Very little in the track record of most large Western companies warrants the confidence of the stock market. Investors aren't hopelessly short-term, they're justifiably skeptical.

We believe that top management's caution reflects a lack of confidence in its own ability to involve the entire organization in revitalization, as opposed to simply raising financial targets. Developing faith in the organization's ability to deliver on tough goals, motivating it to do so, focusing its attention long enough to internalize new capabilities—this is the real challenge for top management. Only by rising to this challenge will senior managers gain the courage they need to commit themselves and their companies to global leadership.

Originally published in July–August 2005. Reprint 6557

Notes

1. Among the first to apply the concept of strategy to management were H. Igor Ansoff in *Corporate Strategy: An Analytic Approach to Business Policy for Growth and Expansion* (McGraw-Hill, 1965) and Kenneth R. Andrews in *The Concept of Corporate Strategy* (Dow Jones-Irwin, 1971).

2. Robert A. Burgelman, "A Process Model of Internal Corporate Venturing in the Diversified Major Firm," *Administrative Science Quarterly,* June 1983.

3. For example, see Michael E. Porter, *Competitive Strategy* (Free Press, 1980).

4. Strategic frameworks for resource allocation in diversified companies are summarized in Charles W. Hofer and Dan E. Schendel, *Strategy Formulation: Analytical Concepts* (West Publishing, 1978).

5. For example, see Peter Lorange and Richard F. Vancil, *Strategic Planning Systems* (Prentice-Hall, 1977).

When Growth Stalls

by Matthew S. Olson, Derek van Bever, and Seth Verry

SENIOR MANAGEMENT AT LEVI STRAUSS & COMPANY could be forgiven for not seeing it coming. The year was 1996. The company had just achieved a personal best, with sales cresting $7 billion for the first time in its history. This performance extended a run of growth in which overall revenue had more than doubled within a decade. Since taking the company private in 1985, management had relaunched the flagship 501 brand, introduced the Dockers line of khaki pants, and increased international sales from 23% to 38% of revenue and more than 50% of profits. Growth in 1995 was the strongest it had been in recent years.

And then came the stall. From that high-water mark of 1996, company sales went into free fall. Year-end revenue results for 2000 were $4.6 billion—a 35% decline from four years prior. Market value declined even more precipitously: Analysts estimate that it went from $14 billion to $8 billion in those four years. The company's share of its core U.S. jeans market dropped by half over the 1990s, falling from 31% in 1990 to 14% by decade's end. Today, with a new management team in place, Levi Strauss has undergone a company-wide transformation. It may be regaining its footing, but it has yet to return to growth.

While more dramatic than many, this is the story of a revenue growth stall—a crisis that can hit even the most exemplary organizations. It shares many elements with other stalls, at companies as varied as 3M, Apple, Banc One, Caterpillar, Daimler-Benz, Toys "R"

No soft landings

An analysis of the growth histories of Fortune 100 and Global 100 companies that experienced stalls between 1955 and 2006 reveals this composite pattern. After a burst of energy, growth does not descend gradually; it drops like a stone.

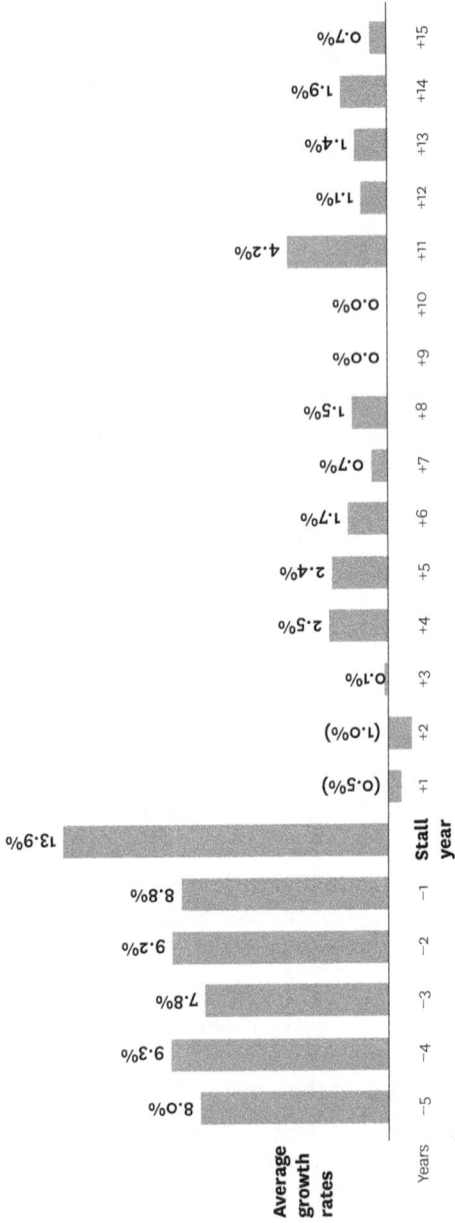

Average growth rates

Years	-5	-4	-3	-2	-1	Stall year	+1	+2	+3	+4	+5	+6	+7	+8	+9	+10	+11	+12	+13	+14	+15
	8.0%	9.3%	7.8%	9.2%	8.8%	13.9%	(0.5%)	(1.0%)	0.1%	2.5%	2.4%	1.7%	0.7%	1.5%	0.0%	0.0%	4.2%	1.1%	1.4%	1.9%	0.7%

Idea in Brief

It happens even to exemplary companies: after years of neck-snapping acceleration in revenue, growth suddenly stalls. And no one saw it coming.

Worse, if executives don't diagnose the cause of a stall and turn things around fast, a company stands little chance of ever returning to healthy top-line growth.

It's tempting to blame stalls on external forces (economic meltdowns, government rulings) and conclude that management is helpless. But according to Olson, Van Bever, and Verry, the most common causes of growth stalls are knowable *and* preventable:

- A premium market position backfires

- Innovation management breaks down

- A core business is abandoned prematurely

- The company lacks a strong talent bench

Understand these causes—along with their telltale clues—and you'll be better equipped to stop your firm from heading into a fatal nosedive.

Us, and Volvo. What these companies would surely recognize in the story is the stall's suddenness. Like Levi Strauss, most organizations actually accelerate into a stall, experiencing unprecedented progress along key measures just before growth rates tumble. When the momentum is lost, it's as if the props have been knocked out from under their corporate strategy. (See the exhibit "No soft landings.") Typically, few on the senior team see the stall coming; core performance metrics often fail to register trouble on the horizon.

As part of our ongoing research into growth, the Corporate Executive Board recently completed a comprehensive analysis of the growth experiences of some 500 leading corporations in the past half century, focusing particularly on "stall points"—our term for the start of secular reversals in company growth fortunes, as opposed to quarterly stumbles or temporary corrections. The companies in our study included more than 400 that have appeared on the *Fortune* 100 since that index was created, some 50 years ago, along with about 90 non-U.S. companies of a similar size. The study revealed patterns in the incidence, costs, and root causes of growth

Idea in Practice

The Four Causes of Growth Stalls

Cause	Explanation	Example	Key Symptoms
Premium position backfires	A company with long-successful premium brands ignores new, low-cost rivals or major shifts in customer preferences.	Levi Strauss ignored the rise of house brands and super-premium designer jeans while its revenues were surging. Its share of the U.S. jeans market dropped by half over the 1990s.	• Market share plummets in narrow customer segments. • Customer acquisition costs jump. • Key customers increasingly resist service enhancements
Innovation management breaks down	A company mismanages the processes for creating new offerings.	After 3M pushed its R&D budget out to its units, the product-centric divisions focused on incremental extensions, not major new offerings. 3M's annual growth rate fell from 17% to 1% between 1979 and 1982.	• Senior executives can't monitor funding decisions at the business-unit level to check the balance between incremental and next-generation investments.
Core business is abandoned prematurely	Believing its core markets are saturated, a company doesn't fully exploit growth opportunities in its existing business.	In the late 1960s, RCA decided the age of break-throughs in consumer electronics had passed. It invested in mainframe computers and acquired consumer-products firms. Meanwhile, Steve Jobs and Bill Gates were on the verge of starting companies that would revolutionize RCA's former core business.	• The company invests in acquisitions or growth initiatives in areas distant from existing customers, products, and channels. • Executives refer to a product line, business unit, or division as "mature."
Company lacks a strong talent bench	The firm has few executives and staff with strategy-execution capabilities.	At Hitachi, executives consistently came up from the company's energy and industrial side, but Hitachi's growth prospects lay elsewhere. No top executives held an MBA or other business degree. In 1994, Hitachi experienced a devastating downward slide in earnings.	• The executive team comprises company lifers with a narrow experience base. • Management development programs focus on replicating current leadership's skills.

Preventing a Stall

Ossified assumptions about customers, competitors, and technologies are the underlying causes of growth stalls. To prevent a stall, surface these assumptions and test their accuracy. Here's how:

- Commission a squad of younger, newer employees to ask questions such as "What industry are we in?" "Who are our customers?"

- Have teams develop visions of your company's future five years hence. Look for issues the scenarios have in common; they reveal core beliefs you should monitor.

- Ask a venture capitalist to sit in on strategy reviews and probe for weaknesses.

stalls. (Our research approach is described briefly in the sidebar "The Search for Stall Points.")

On the quantitative record alone, we can attest that Levi Strauss is in good company: 87% of the companies in this group have suffered one or more stall points. We can also appreciate the consequences of such events. On average, companies lose 74% of their market capitalization, as measured against the S&P 500 index, in the decade surrounding a growth stall. More often than not, the CEO and senior team are replaced in its aftermath. And unless management is able to diagnose the causes of a stall and get the company back on track quickly—turning it around in a matter of several years—the odds are against its ever returning to healthy top-line growth.

Deeper analysis sheds light on the most common causes of growth stalls, which turn out to be preventable for the most part. There is

The Search for Stall Points

TO UNDERSTAND THE PREVALENCE of serious growth crises in large companies, as well as their costs and causes, we analyzed the experiences of more than 400 companies that have been listed on the *Fortune* 100 since its inception, in 1955, and of about 90 comparable non-U.S. companies. Some 500 companies over 50 years gave us 25,000 years' worth of historical data and information to mine for insights. A pattern that emerged from these histories yielded the useful construct of the stall point—that moment when a company's growth rate slips into what proves to be a prolonged decline.

We began by analyzing the revenue growth records of every company in our study to identify which companies had experienced stall points and when. Specifically, we calculated the compound annual growth rate (CAGR) of each company's revenue for 10 years before and 10 years after every year in the past half-century for which data were available. To qualify as having stalled in a given year, a company must have enjoyed compound annual growth of at least 2% in real dollars for the 10-year period prior to the potential stall point; the difference in CAGR for the 10 years preceding and the 10 years following must have been at least four percentage points; and the CAGR of the subsequent 10 years must have fallen below 6% in real dollars. One stall point identified in this manner is shown below.

We then turned our attention to *why* companies stall. Out of the 500 companies, we selected for in-depth case research 50 that were representative of the whole in terms of industry mix and age. We assembled comprehensive dossiers on all of them, drawing on the public record of financial reports and published materials, on case studies, and on personal interviews. This enabled us to identify the top three factors contributing to each company's growth stall. After all these analyses we were able to identify the root causes of stalls and the major categories they fell into. We arrived at our framework purely inductively, from the bottom up. (See "The root causes of revenue stalls.")

Readers may be wondering why we chose revenue rather than profit, value, or some other measure on which to focus our analysis. That is a fair question, and we considered our choice at length. It rests on two premises. The first is that revenue growth, more than any other metric, is the primary driver of long-term company performance. This is not to say that revenue growth without profits is desirable, but high growth through margin management alone is unsustainable. The second premise is more mundane: It's hard to manipulate the top line over time, and market value and profit measures are much more variable. Revenue growth guided us to the most meaningful turning points in corporate growth history.

One company's stall point

Tracking the growth of the BF Goodrich Corporation over a 20-year period, we can clearly see its stall point. Annual growth rates are shown for a decade before and a decade after what proved to be the stall year. The turning point in Goodrich's fortunes came in 1979, after which the company's growth fell into secular decline.

Year	1974	1975	1976	1977	1978	**1979**	1980	1981	1982	1983	1984
CAGR 10 years prior	3.7%	1.4%	1.0%	2.1%	2.2%	**2.5%**	2.7%	2.3%	(0.4%)	(0.6%)	(1.1%)
CAGR 10 years after	(1.1%)	(0.9%)	(3.2%)	(5.5%)	(5.6%)	**(6.5%)**	(6.2%)	(5.9%)	(4.8%)	(8.3%)	(7.1%)
Difference	4.8%	2.3%	4.2%	7.6%	7.8%	**9.0%**	8.9%	8.2%	4.4%	7.7%	6.0%

a common assumption that when the fortunes of great companies plunge, it must be owing to big, external forces—economic meltdowns, acts of God, or government rulings—for which management cannot be held accountable. In fact most stalls occur for reasons that are both knowable and addressable at the time. The exhibit "The root causes of revenue stalls" reveals the factors that lay behind the stalls of 50 companies we went on to study in depth; clearly, a company can falter in many ways. One might almost think that sustaining growth in a very large company depends on doing absolutely everything right. But the root causes of stalls are not so varied or complex that we can't see patterns.

What the exhibit demonstrates is that the vast majority of stall factors result from a choice about strategy or organizational design. They are, in other words, controllable by management. Further, even within this broad realm, nearly half of all root causes fall into one of four categories: premium-position captivity, innovation management breakdown, premature core abandonment, and talent bench shortfall.

In this article we'll offer advice for avoiding these hazards, drawing from practices currently in use at large, high-growth companies to foresee possible stalls and head them off. More generally we will explore why management is so often blindsided by these events. As we will show, a large number of global companies may at this moment be perilously close to their own stall points. Knowing how to avoid growth stalls begins with understanding their causes. Let's look at each of the four categories.

When a Premium Position Backfires

By far the largest category of factors responsible for serious revenue stalls is what we have labeled premium-position captivity: the inability of a firm to respond effectively to new, low-cost competitive challenges or to a significant shift in customer valuation of product features.

We use the term "captivity" because it suggests how management teams can be hemmed in by a long history of success. A company that solidly occupies a premium market position remains insulated longer than its competitors against evolution in the external environment. It has less reason to doubt its business model, which has historically provided a competitive advantage, and once it perceives the crisis, it changes too little too late. When the towering strengths of a firm are transformed into towering weaknesses, it's a cruel reversal.

Readers will recognize the intellectual kinship between our notion of premium-position captivity and the patterns of technology disruption described by Clayton M. Christensen in his landmark book *The Innovator's Dilemma* (Harvard Business School Press, 1997). As we scan the broad data set of the *Fortune* 100 over the past half century, we are struck by Christensen's acumen. In documenting premium-position captivity in leading enterprises, we saw a cycle of disdain, denial, and rationalization that kept many management teams from responding meaningfully to market changes.

Price and quality leaders such as Eastman Kodak and Caterpillar, for example, have found themselves unable (or unwilling) to formulate a timely, effective response to the threat posed by foreign entrants. The owners of iconic brands, such as American Express, Heinz, and Procter & Gamble, may assume that the decades-long investments they have made in their brands will protect their premium prices against lower-cost entrants. Both Compaq and Philip Morris (now part of Altria) failed to respond to signs of trouble in the early 1990s because they relied on performance metrics designed around generous margins.

We saw premium-position captivity at work in the Levi Strauss stall when the company failed to spot a strategic inflection in customer demand. In cases like this one, organizations and their multiple sophisticated market-sensing activities simply don't recognize the importance of an emerging behavior or customer preference in their core markets. They continue to place their bets on product or service attributes that are in decline, while disruptive entrants emphasizing different, underrecognized features gain ground.

In the early 1990s Levi Strauss enjoyed surging revenues even as its relationships with the Gap and other distributors faltered and as

The root causes of revenue stalls

A careful analysis of 50 representative companies that experienced growth stalls revealed nearly as many root causes for them: 42 external, strategic, and organizational factors, which can be grouped into categories as shown here. We identified the top three factors contributing to each company's stall and considered those results as a whole in determining how large a role (indicated by percentage) each category played. The clustering that is at the heart of our findings is clear: Four categories account for more than half the occurrences of root causes we cataloged—premium-position captivity, innovation management breakdown, premature core abandonment, and talent bench shortfall.

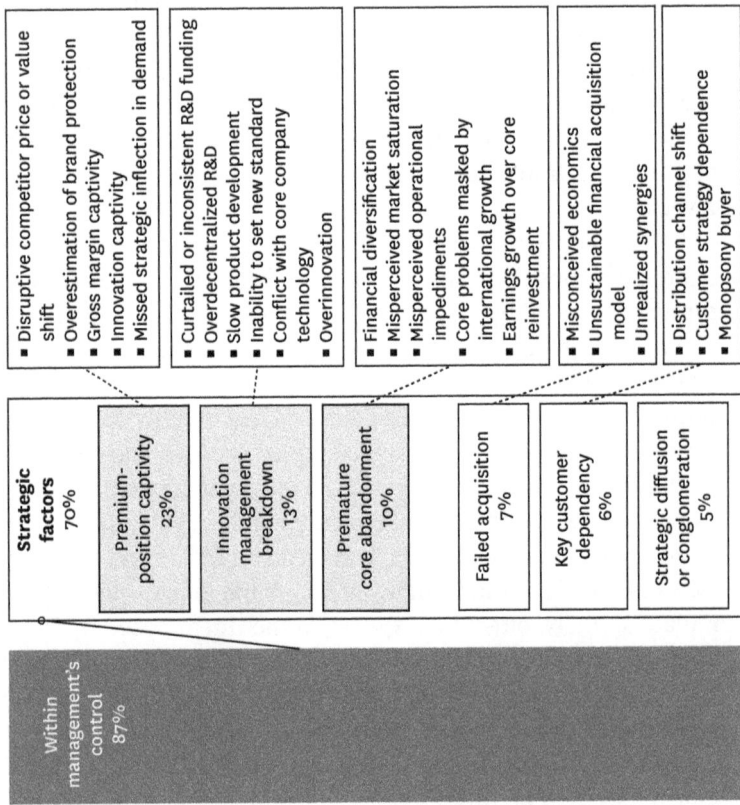

Within management's control 87%	Strategic factors 70%	
	Premium-position captivity 23%	■ Disruptive competitor price or value shift ■ Overestimation of brand protection ■ Gross margin captivity ■ Innovation captivity ■ Missed strategic inflection in demand
	Innovation management breakdown 13%	■ Curtailed or inconsistent R&D funding ■ Overdecentralized R&D ■ Slow product development ■ Inability to set new standard ■ Conflict with core company technology ■ Overinnovation
	Premature core abandonment 10%	■ Financial diversification ■ Misperceived market saturation ■ Misperceived operational impediments ■ Core problems masked by international growth ■ Earnings growth over core reinvestment
	Failed acquisition 7%	■ Misconceived economics ■ Unsustainable financial acquisition model ■ Unrealized synergies
	Key customer dependency 6%	■ Distribution channel shift ■ Customer strategy dependence ■ Monopsony buyer
	Strategic diffusion or conglomeration 5%	

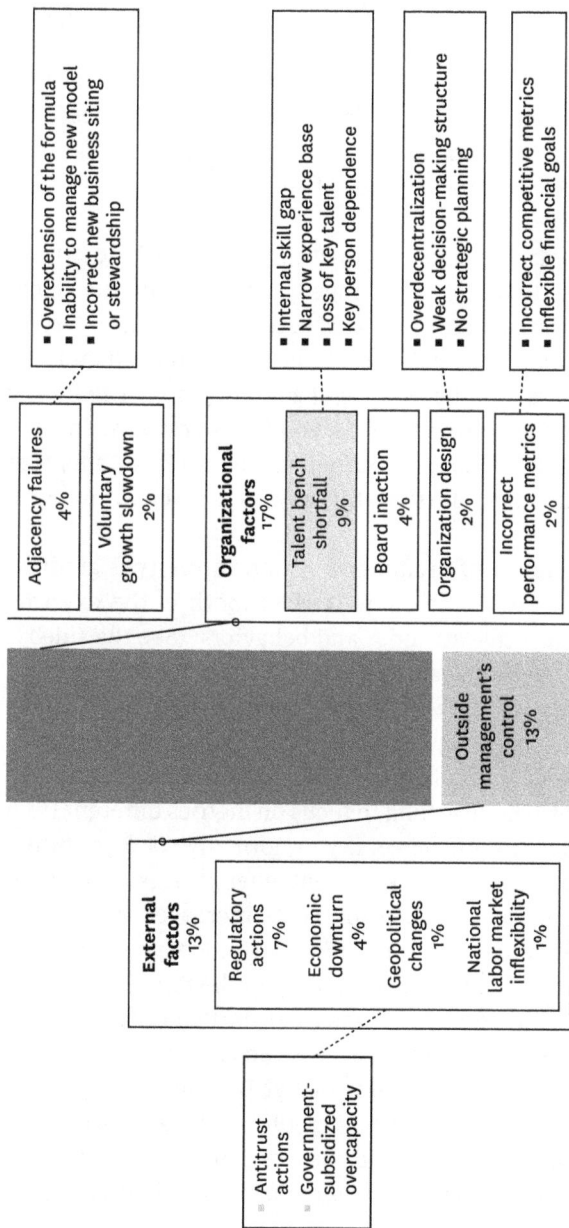

External factors
13%

Regulatory actions
7%

Economic downturn
4%

Geopolitical changes
1%

National labor market inflexibility
1%

- Antitrust actions
- Government-subsidized overcapacity

Outside management's control
13%

Adjacency failures
4%

Voluntary growth slowdown
2%

- Overextension of the formula
- Inability to manage new model
- Incorrect new business siting or stewardship

Organizational factors
17%

Talent bench shortfall
9%

- Internal skill gap
- Narrow experience base
- Loss of key talent
- Key person dependence

Board inaction
4%

Organization design
2%

- Overdecentralization
- Weak decision-making structure
- No strategic planning

Incorrect performance metrics
2%

- Incorrect competitive metrics
- Inflexible financial goals

designers and retailers introduced jeans products at the high and low ends of the market. The rise of house brands and superpremium designer jeans looked manageable—or ignorable—as long as healthy revenue growth continued. By the time the growth stall had become evident, the company found itself with an expensive retailing strategy and a product line that was out of step with both ends of the denim jeans market.

The market data relating to this growth stall were not hidden from Levi Strauss executives; the challenge was to separate the signal from the noise. The company's years of success warped its interpretation of what it was seeing. Its story illustrates how difficult it is to respond to a threat in the absence of a burning platform: If your sales are continuing to rise, how do you focus concern? In 1999 Gordon Shank, then the company's chief marketing officer, admitted ruefully, "We didn't read the signs that all was not well. Or we were in denial."

Although the onset of premium-position captivity is gradual, there are often clues that trouble is afoot, both in the external market and in executive attitudes and behaviors. (See the sidebar "When Does a Premium Position Become a Trap?") Easiest to spot in marketing data are pockets of rapid market share loss, particularly in narrow customer segments, and increasing resistance among key customers to solutions wrappers and other bundling of services. It can also be revealing to focus on metrics different from those you ordinarily emphasize. If you normally track profit per customer, for example, you are content when it rises. But would you notice if customer acquisition costs increased even more rapidly? When it comes to management attitudes, your ears may pick up the strongest clues: Listen closely to the tone in the executive suite when conversation turns to upstart competitors or to successful rivals that are viewed as less capable. Is it acceptable, or routine, to dismiss them as unworthy? Do your processes for gathering intelligence about your competitors ignore some of these market participants because of their size or perceived lack of quality? Indulging in such behavior is common, but it's a luxury that no market leader can afford.

When Innovation Management Breaks Down

The second most frequent cause of growth stalls is what we call innovation management breakdown: some chronic problem in managing the internal business processes for updating existing products and services and creating new ones. We saw manifestations of this at every major stage along the activity chain of product innovation, from basic research and development to product commercialization.

Where revenue growth stalls could be attributed to innovation breakdown, the problems emphatically did not center on individual product launch failures; a New Coke may occasionally belly flop, but the result is typically a temporary growth stumble rather than a fateful turning point in a company's growth history. By contrast, the secular growth stalls we identified were attributable to systemic inefficiencies or dysfunctions. Given that most large corporations rely on business models that have evolved to generate sequential product innovations, when things go wrong here—at the heart of these organizations' most important business process—extremely serious, multiyear problems result.

For firms shifting the bulk of their R&D activities out to their business units, our case studies provide a strong cautionary tale. The logic behind such shifts is clear: The closer R&D is to markets and individual unit strategies, the higher its return on investment should be. But problems seem to arise when decentralization is combined with an explicit (or implicit) metric that demands a high share of revenue growth from new-product introductions. The result can be an overallocation of resources to ever smaller incremental product opportunities, at the expense of sustained R&D investment in larger, future product platforms.

A stark example of this occurred at 3M in the 1970s, when the company experienced a revenue stall after decades of robust top-line growth. Since its founding, in 1902, 3M had followed a clear formula for success, developing innovative products with industrial applications that supported a premium position and then leapfrogging to the next opportunity as the market matured. This strategy, which

When Does a Premium Position Become a Trap?

AT THE TOP OF EVERY industry are companies that have built premium positions for themselves, dominating the market among the most demanding customer segments and providing products or services that lead the field in performance, thus commanding higher prices. The organizational strengths in product development, brand management, and marketing that created these top positions are sources of great pride to the firms that cultivated them.

But attack from new competitors with significantly lower cost structures, or changes in customer preferences that start slowly and then reach tipping points, can actually transform these dependable sources of competitive advantage into weaknesses. Product innovation loses its ability to protect pricing premiums, and presumed brand and marketing strengths no longer dependably protect market share. All the firm's business processes and activities, developed and honed for the top end of the market, become impediments to refreshing strategy.

It is possible to spot the onset of premium-position captivity. The six yes-or-no questions below probe awareness of threatening market dynamics, an executive team's blind spots regarding competitive threats, and intelligence capabilities for recognizing an impending encroachment on premium turf.

Clues in Market Dynamics

- Are we losing market share to nonpremium rivals in subsegments of our markets?

has been characterized as "the corporate millipede" ("Make a little, sell a little, make a little more"), had by the early 1970s produced a portfolio of more than 60,000 products (the majority of them with sales under $100 million), while more than 25% of total corporate sales came from products less than five years old.

The growth potential inherent in this niche-jumping strategy began to dwindle in the late 1970s, as the firm approached $5 billion in revenue. With the recession of the early 1980s looming, 3M management decided to hold R&D expenditures below historical

- Are key customers increasingly resistant to paying price premiums for product enhancements?

Clues in Executive Team Attitudes

- Does the senior executive team resist the proposition that nonpremium players operate in the same business or product category that we do?

- Do we commonly dismiss the possibility that nonpremium rivals and low-end entrants will penetrate the upper ends of our markets?

Clues in Market and Competitor Research

- Do we fail to track shifts in secondary and tertiary customer-group behavior with the same rigor we use for our higher-end segments?

- Do we exclude nonpremium players and low-end entrants from our tracking of competitive threats?

A "yes" to two or more of these questions suggests the need to refocus research into markets and competitors. The goal should be to map premium features and low-end competitor performance. A "yes" to four or more suggests an immediate need for contingency planning: How might the firm modify its current business model (including its margin requirements and cost basis) to respond to a low-cost entrant within 18 months?

averages of just over 6% of annual sales and to push most of the R&D budget down to the company's 42 divisions (usually organized around individual product lines).

Total growth slowed as divisions focused on ever narrower niche-segment opportunities. From 1979 to 1982 the company saw its annual growth rate fall from 17% to just over 1%, with sales per employee creeping downward simultaneously. Because the bulk of R&D was controlled by product-centric business units, major new-product development activity was replaced by incremental product line extensions. The former CEO Allen F. Jacobson observed of that era, "Historically, our drive for profit and our preference for developing premium-priced products aimed at market niches meant that we were not comfortable competing only on price. As a result, we never fully developed our manufacturing competencies. And when competitors followed us, we would refuse to confront them—it was always easier to innovate our way into a new niche."

As we looked at the variety of ways in which problems in the innovation management process can eventually produce major revenue stalls, we were struck by the fragility of this chain of activities, and by how vulnerable the whole process is to management decisions made to achieve perfectly valid corporate goals. There are some powerful clues, however, when a company is at serious risk. Most significant is probably not the overall level of R&D spending but how those dollars are being spent. Is the senior team able to look into funding decisions at the business unit level to monitor the balance between incremental and next-generation investments? Are R&D and other innovation resources at the corporate level budgeted separately from incremental innovation? Is some portion of innovation funding allocated to creating lower-cost versions of existing products and services? Given the long lead times characteristic of the innovation process, flaws are slow to surface—and time-consuming to remedy.

When a Core Business Is Abandoned

The third major cause of revenue stalls is premature core abandonment: the failure to fully exploit growth opportunities in the existing core business. Its telltale markers are acquisitions or growth initiatives in areas relatively distant from existing customers, products, and channels.

This category has received significant attention in the recent business literature. Perhaps as a result, stalls attributed to premature core abandonment cluster in the period before 1990. We are tempted to credit the management consulting industry for having hammered home the need for attention to core businesses. In particular, Chris Zook, of Bain & Company, has stayed on this issue with ferocity.

That is not to say that *Fortune* 100–size firms have mastered the art of generating continuous growth in their core businesses. Quite the contrary: The recent wave of private equity takeovers suggests that many public companies still struggle in their efforts to grow established businesses. Almost without exception, these take-overs are based on strategies for growing the core—strategies that public-company executive teams are either unable or unwilling to pursue.

The two most common mistakes we saw in this category were believing that one's core markets are saturated and viewing operational impediments in the core business model as a signal to move on to new, presumably easier competitive terrain. Either situation invariably ended badly, with some competitor moving in to displace the incumbent.

In the late 1960s Robert Sarnoff, the CEO of RCA and son of David Sarnoff, the legendary force behind the company, came to the mistaken belief that "the age of the big breakthroughs in consumer electronics—the age in which [his father] had built RCA—had passed." James Hillier, the head of the company's labs, asserted, "The physicists have discovered about all they are going to for consumer application in the near future."

One can hardly blame Sarnoff when even the physicists were advocating moving on—and move on he did. He pursued initiatives in three new, presumably higher-growth directions. First, mainframe computers seemed a logical choice, given that technology-driven big bets had powered RCA's growth since the 1920s. Second, he decided that marketing was the future and deployed huge resources to acquire companies in the consumer products sector. Third, the company redirected internal resources from consumer electronics research into marketing and brand management projects. Meanwhile, Steve Jobs and Bill Gates were on the road to starting companies that would launch a revolution in RCA's former core markets.

Just as interesting as getting it wrong on core business growth prospects is the tendency of executive teams to simply give up on apparently intractable problems in their core businesses. The most intriguing example of this occurred at Kmart. A highly successful challenger to Sears as a general-merchandise big-box retailer, Kmart relentlessly stole its formerly indomitable competitor's market share through the 1960s and 1970s.

In 1976 Kmart reached a peak in new store openings, adding 271 facilities to its countrywide network. That would prove to be its limit. Over the next decade the company reined in expansion in its core business, convinced that the U.S. market was saturated. Its chairman, Robert Dewar, created a special strategy group whose purpose was to study new growth avenues and, in the parlance of the time, far-out ideas. He also established a performance goal for the company: 25% of sales should come from new ventures by 1990.

What's most disturbing about Kmart's choices is not that management was tempted to diversify in search of growth—however misguided this appears in hindsight, given Wal-Mart's concurrent gathering of strength. Rather, it is that the executive team failed to monitor and match the distribution and inventory management capabilities that its rival was pioneering in Bentonville, Arkansas. In the early 1980s, while Wal-Mart was installing its first point-of-service system with a satellite link for automatic reorders, Kmart was acquiring Furr's Cafeterias of Texas, the Bishop's Buffet chain, and pizza-video parlors as outlets for its retained earnings. Throughout the next decade Wal-Mart continued to invest in its cross-docking distribution system, while Kmart pursued a range of disparate businesses, including PayLess Drug Stores, the Sports Authority, and OfficeMax. By the end of the 1980s Kmart was at least 10 years behind Wal-Mart in its logistical capabilities, handing Wal-Mart a "gimme" advantage of more than 1% of sales in inbound logistics costs. As Kmart lagged ever further behind, its imagined need for outside-the-core growth platforms became real.

Of all the red flags signaling stall risk, one of the most obvious is management's use of the term "mature" to refer to any of its product lines, business units, or divisions. (The disinvestment in the core implied by the "cash cow" cell of the growth-share matrix does modern managers no favor.) Established businesses should be managed against significant revenue and earnings goals, and business leaders should actively explore the potential of new business models to rejuvenate even the most "mature" businesses.

When Talent Comes Up Short

Our fourth major category is talent bench shortfall: a lack of leaders and staff with the skills and capabilities required for strategy execution.

Talent bench shortfall merits careful definition, because it has become a fact of daily life in many industries and functions. Indeed, at this writing, shortages of critical talent are the primary concern of human resources departments globally, not just in high-growth markets but in a range of specialty skill categories, and they are expected to get worse. What stops growth dead in its tracks, however, is not merely a shortage of talent but the absence of required capabilities— such as solutions-selling skills or consumer-marketing expertise—in key areas of a company, most visibly at the executive level.

Internal skill gaps are often self-inflicted wounds, the unintended consequence of promote-from-within policies that have been too strictly applied. Such policies, often most fervent in organizations with strong cultures, can accelerate growth in the heady early days of executing a successful business model. But when the external environment presents novel challenges, or competition intensifies, these policies may be a severe drag on progress.

One important element in this category is a narrow experience base at the senior executive level that prevents a timely response to emerging strategic issues. The most common marker of this lack of experience is managers' tendency to follow a well-worn internal path from a dominant business, market, or function to the executive suite. Hitachi, which went into a growth stall in 1994, illustrates this problem. At the time, Hitachi accounted for 2% of Japan's GNP and 6% of its corporate R&D spending. The downward slide in the company's revenue was devastating. Executive management has consistently come up from the energy and industrial side of the company, but Hitachi's growth prospects lie elsewhere. This narrowness extends to functional pedigree: The firm has historically had an engineering culture, with none of its top executives holding an MBA or other business degree. As Hitachi looks toward its centennial in 2010, however, change may be in the offing: Kazuo Furukawa, who was named president and chief operating officer in 2006, came up through the telecom and information systems sectors. He is the company's first president with no exposure to its heavy electrical machinery business.

Few companies formally monitor the balance in the executive team between company lifers and newer hires who offer fresh perspectives and approaches. Furthermore, large companies have a fairly poor track record on incorporating new voices into senior management. Most studies agree that 35% to 40% of senior hires wash out within their first 18 months—a statistic that is improving glacially as we adopt new practices in talent management. And management development programs all too often focus on replicating the skill sets of the current leadership, rather than on developing the novel skills and perspectives that tomorrow's leaders will need to overcome evolving challenges.

We have identified a simple way to ensure balance in the senior executive ranks—what we call mix management. Our analysis of company growth rates and senior leaders' backgrounds suggests that the sweet spot for external talent is somewhere between 10% and 30% of senior management. That is a good target for the CEO and the board to use with the firm's executive committee and for human resources to use with the top 5% of the workforce.

When What You Know Is No Longer So

As noted, the four categories we have outlined account for nearly half of all the root causes we cataloged. A host of other, less common causes that came up in our analysis crossed a broad terrain, including failed acquisitions, key customer dependency, strategic diffusion, adjacency failures, and voluntary growth slowdowns. A powerful observation can be distilled from this array: One culprit in all our case studies was management's failure to bring the underlying assumptions that drive company strategy into line with changes in the external environment—whether because of a lack of awareness that the gap existed or was widening, or because of faulty prioritization.

The lack of awareness is particularly vexing, because it is so insidious. Strategic assumptions begin life as observations about customers, competitors, or technologies that arise from direct experience. They are then enshrined in the strategic plan and translated into operational guidance. Eventually they harden into orthodoxy. This explains why, when we examine individual case studies, we so often find that those assumptions the team has held the longest or the most deeply are the likeliest to be its undoing. Some beliefs have come to appear so obvious that it is no longer politic to debate them.

Part of the reason that few top teams question assumptions is that doing so goes against the nature of the senior executive mandate: The CEO and his or her executive team are paid to develop a vision and execute it—with resolve. Another part is human nature: Introspection and self-doubt don't often appear in the personality profiles of top executives at large enterprises. A third part is process: CEOs have very few opportunities to safely express their midnight anxieties. And the one opportunity for stock taking that is built into the annual calendar of most firms—the review of the strategic plan for the coming year—all too often fails to stimulate deep, searching conversation. Indeed, the "assumptions and risks" section of virtually all strategic plan templates is generally treated as a pro forma exercise rather than an occasion to go deep.

Articulating and Testing Strategic Assumptions

To assist executives in spotting signs of vulnerability to growth stalls in their own organizations, we offer two kinds of tools. The first is a diagnostic self-test we developed at the conclusion of our research. Hoping to determine how companies might foresee a stall, our team spent considerable time looking at various financial metrics, from margin erosion to patterns in R&D spending. This effort was fruitless: Financial metrics—at least those available to the public—are as likely to lag behind as lead an organization's change in strategic vitality.

Red Flags for Growth Stalls

ARE YOU ABOUT TO HIT a stall point? A diagnostic survey of 50 red flags can help signal the danger in time. Below is a sampling of red flags relating to premium-position captivity; other parts of the survey highlight other hazards. To the extent that your senior team and high-potential managers see these as areas for concern, you may be headed for a free fall.

- Our core assumptions about the marketplace and about the capabilities that are critical to support our strategy are not written down.

- We haven't revisited our market definition boundaries, and therefore our list of current and emerging competitors, in several years.

- We haven't refreshed our working definition of our core market, and therefore our understanding of our market share, in several years.

- We test only infrequently for shifts in key customer groups' valuation of our product/service attributes.

- We are less effective than our competitors at translating customer insights into new product and service categories.

- Core customers are increasingly unwilling to pay a premium for our brand reputation or superior performance.

To watch the authors discuss their complete list of red flags and how to use them to diagnose impending growth stalls, go to stallpoints.multimedia.hbr.org.

What we did find helpful was asking, What could the company's senior managers have seen in their markets, in their competitors' behavior, in their own internal practices, that might have alerted them to an impending stall? We looked at our detailed case histories for warning signs before the stall point that perhaps hadn't received the scrutiny they deserved, and uncovered 50 red flags, all rooted in the real experience of the companies we studied. Our 20/20 hindsight may enable you to spot signs faster in your own organization. (See the sidebar "Red Flags for Growth Stalls.")

Also included in our tool kit are four practices drawn from those we've seen management teams use. The first two are effective in making strategic assumptions explicit, and the latter two are designed to test those assumptions for ongoing relevance and accuracy. A hallmark of these practices is that they are embedded in the work flow of the firm—the job of some individual or team—or other-wise built into core operating systems.

Commission a core-belief identification squad

This practice is simple to execute and involves calling on a diverse, cross-functional working group to go hunting for the firm's most deeply held assumptions about itself and the industry in which it operates. (Gary Hamel and his colleagues at Strategos have led the way on this practice.) The best-functioning squads include a significant share of younger, newer employees, who are less likely to be invested in current orthodoxies. Their efforts are most fruitful when the team is prepared to raise thorny issues and challenge entrenched beliefs, using methods ranging from reality checks—What industry are we in? Who are our customers?—to more provocative explorations: What 10 things would you never hear customers say about our business? Which firms have succeeded by breaking the established "rules" of the industry? What conventions did they overturn?

One leading consumer-goods company told us that it had used this practice to kick off an inquiry into long-term growth pathways and to challenge conventions that had taken hold through the years. We like the practice for two reasons. First, it seems to strike the right balance between traditional, closed-door strategy discussions and all-company "jams," which tend to lose credibility and edge in direct proportion to the number of participants involved. Second, it manages to simultaneously address areas of universal agreement and issues that are in play.

Conduct a premortem strategic analysis

Many leaders have found it useful to charge teams with developing competing visions of the future success—or failure—of the company as it would be reported in a business periodical five years hence. (See Gary Klein, "Performing a Project *Pre*mortem," Forethought, HBR September 2007.) The process typically takes place over one or two days at regularly scheduled offsite management gatherings, and teams senior executives with high-potential staffers from around the world. By seeing which issues the scenarios have in common, leadership teams can identify the subset of core beliefs that should be most closely examined and monitored.

Appoint a shadow cabinet

Pioneered by a *Fortune* 250 manufacturing company, the shadow cabinet is a standing group of high-potential employees who tend to be in midcareer and are often in line for promotion to the director level. They usually meet the day before an executive committee meeting, and their agenda matches as closely as possible the agenda for the following day, with presenters delivering dry runs of their material to the group and then providing whatever follow-up is needed to support the group's deliberations and decision making. The members of the shadow cabinet are invited to executive committee meetings on a rotating basis.

The benefits of this practice are manifold. Because it provides such powerful seasoning for the employees who participate, it becomes a mainstay of the leadership development curriculum. And because senior executives are usually most attached to the assumptions underlying current strategy (it is *their* strategy, after all), they find the fresh perspectives offered by this creditable, well-informed constituency extremely valuable. That said, most executives to whom we've presented this idea respond that it would never work in their organizations. "The executive agenda is too confidential," they say, or "Our executive team is too impatient," or "It looks like too much work." We agree that this practice is not for everyone; in fact, we have visited boardrooms where speaking candidly about shortcomings in company strategy would be a truly career-limiting move. Organizations where this is the case should pass on the idea. Not only will it fail to achieve the desired effect but it may cause more harm than good to the morale of staff members involved in the initiative.

Invite a venture capitalist to your strategy review

An effective way to bring an external perspective to bear on strategy assumptions is to ask a qualified venture capitalist to sit in on business unit strategy and investment reviews and probe for potential weaknesses. The benefits for business unit managers come primarily from specific challenges but more generally from the practical, payback-focused lens that the VC brings to the review. What's more, the impact of the venture capitalist approach can live on well after the exercise. (Recording all the questions and methods the VC uses to gather information will preserve the essentials of the approach for later reuse.)

The obvious difficulty in implementing this practice is identifying an external party who is knowledgeable enough to add value to the conversation but "safe" enough to be allowed in the room. (In the current climate, representatives from the private equity community might easily meet the first requirement but miserably fail the second.) The organization that brought this idea to our attention was coventuring with a VC and so had begun to build some operating trust.

Unlike corporate investors, VCs are accustomed to serving on the boards of portfolio companies; acting in a similar capacity for a corporate partner isn't much of a stretch. For the corporate partner, however, the experience can be nothing short of eye-opening. The VC's perspective provides an in-the-moment test of assumptions about markets, customers, and competitors and brings an urgency to corporate processes that often feel routine. Deliberation around investment proposals takes on a very different tone. For a venture capitalist, each decision to fund is optional; the usual approach is to release additional funding only when meaningful milestones have been achieved. Freedom to operate for a quarter—not a year—is the norm.

Renewing Competence in Strategy

The practices we recommend in this article compete for space on an already overcrowded executive agenda. What gives force to our advocacy is that growth stalls can have dire consequences: They bring down even the most admired companies; they exact a sizable financial and human toll; and their impact may be permanent. After a stall sets in, the odds against recovery rise dramatically with the passage of time. (See the exhibit "The long-term effects of stalls.")

The long-term effects of stalls

Fortune 100 and Global 100 Companies, 1955–2006

The overwhelming majority (87%) of companies in our study had experienced a stall. Fewer than half of those (46%) were able to return to moderate or high growth within the decade. When slow growth was allowed to persist for more than 10 years, the delay was most often fatal: Only 7% of the companies in that category ever returned to moderate or high growth.

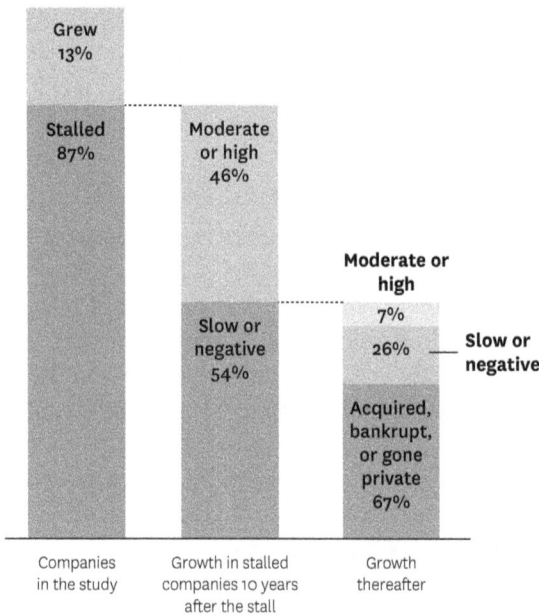

Grew
13%

Stalled
87%

Moderate
or high
46%

Moderate or
high

7%

Slow or
negative
54%

26% — Slow or
negative

Acquired,
bankrupt,
or gone
private
67%

| Companies in the study | Growth in stalled companies 10 years after the stall | Growth thereafter |

Compounding this urgency, all signs point to an increasing risk of stalls in the near future. Of particular concern today is the shrinking half-life of established business models. The importance of spotting change early enough to react in time is rising exponentially. The practices we outline here create that early-warning capability. As critical, they make the strategy conversation ongoing, rather than once a quarter or once a year, and charge line managers at all levels of the firm with leading that conversation. Clay Christensen argued in these pages a decade ago that competent strategic thinking was atrophying in the executive suite because it occurred so infrequently relative to other regular activities. (See "Making Strategy: Learning by Doing," HBR November–December 1997.) As students of strategy-making in large corporations since then, we have found that the problem has only worsened.

Whatever other concerns are on the strategy agenda, guarding against growth stalls should be at the top. The tools we offer will enable the executive team to continually test the accuracy of its worldview and to flag any flawed assumptions that might trigger a stall if they go uncorrected. We know of no more powerful investment for managing controllable risk.

Originally published in March 2008. Reprint R0803C

The Secrets to Successful Strategy Execution

by Gary L. Neilson, Karla L. Martin, and Elizabeth Powers

A BRILLIANT STRATEGY, BLOCKBUSTER PRODUCT, or breakthrough technology can put you on the competitive map, but only solid execution can keep you there. You have to be able to deliver on your intent. Unfortunately, the majority of companies aren't very good at it, by their own admission. Over the past five years, we have invited many thousands of employees (about 25% of whom came from executive ranks) to complete an online assessment of their organizations' capabilities, a process that's generated a database of 125,000 profiles representing more than 1,000 companies, government agencies, and not-for-profits in over 50 countries. Employees at three out of every five companies rated their organization weak at execution—that is, when asked if they agreed with the statement "Important strategic and operational decisions are quickly translated into action," the majority answered no.

Execution is the result of thousands of decisions made every day by employees acting according to the information they have and their own self-interest. In our work helping more than 250 companies learn to execute more effectively, we've identified four fundamental building blocks executives can use to influence those actions—clarifying decision rights, designing information flows, aligning motivators, and making changes to structure. (For simplicity's sake we refer to them as decision rights, information, motivators, and structure.)

In efforts to improve performance, most organizations go right to structural measures because moving lines around the org chart seems the most obvious solution and the changes are visible and concrete. Such steps generally reap some short-term efficiencies quickly, but in so doing address only the symptoms of dysfunction, not its root causes. Several years later, companies usually end up in the same place they started. Structural change can and should be part of the path to improved execution, but it's best to think of it as the capstone, not the cornerstone, of any organizational transformation. In fact, our research shows that actions having to do with decision rights and information are far more important—about twice as effective—as improvements made to the other two building blocks. (See the exhibit "What matters most to strategy execution.")

Take, for example, the case of a global consumer packaged-goods company that lurched down the reorganization path in the early 1990s. (We have altered identifying details in this and other cases

What matters most to strategy execution

When a company fails to execute its strategy, the first thing managers often think to do is restructure. But our research shows that the fundamentals of good execution start with clarifying decision rights and making sure information flows where it needs to go. If you get those right, the correct structure and motivators often become obvious.

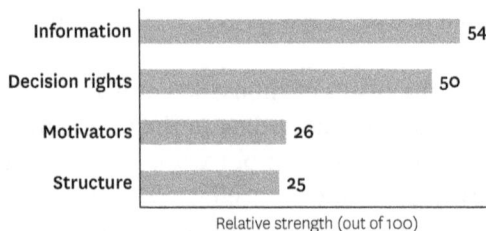

Information — 54
Decision rights — 50
Motivators — 26
Structure — 25

Relative strength (out of 100)

Idea in Brief

A brilliant strategy may put you on the competitive map. But only solid execution keeps you there. Unfortunately, most companies struggle with implementation. That's because they overrely on structural changes, such as reorganization, to execute their strategy.

Though structural change has its place in execution, it produces only short-term gains. For example, one company reduced its management layers as part of a strategy to address disappointing performance. Costs plummeted initially, but the layers soon crept back in.

Research by Neilson, Martin, and Powers shows that execution exemplars focus their efforts on two levers far more powerful than structural change:

- **Clarifying decision rights—** for instance, specifying who "owns" each decision and who must provide input

- **Ensuring information flows where it's needed**—such as promoting managers laterally so they build networks needed for the cross-unit collaboration critical to a new strategy

Tackle decision rights and information flows first, and only then **alter organizational structures** and **realign incentives** to *support* those moves.

that follow.) Disappointed with company performance, senior management did what most companies were doing at that time: They restructured. They eliminated some layers of management and broadened spans of control. Management-staffing costs quickly fell by 18%. Eight years later, however, it was déjà vu. The layers had crept back in, and spans of control had once again narrowed. In addressing only structure, management had attacked the visible symptoms of poor performance but not the underlying cause—how people made decisions and how they were held accountable.

This time, management looked beyond lines and boxes to the mechanics of how work got done. Instead of searching for ways to strip out costs, they focused on improving execution—and in the process discovered the true reasons for the performance shortfall. Managers didn't have a clear sense of their respective roles and responsibilities. They did not intuitively understand which decisions were theirs to make. Moreover, the link between performance

Idea in Practice

The following levers matter *most* for successful strategy execution:

Decision Rights

- Ensure that everyone in your company knows which decisions and actions they're responsible for.

  Example: In one global consumer-goods company, decisions made by divisional and geographic leaders were overridden by corporate functional leaders who controlled resource allocations. Decisions stalled. Overhead costs mounted as divisions added staff to create bulletproof cases for challenging corporate decisions. To support a new strategy hinging on sharper customer focus, the CEO designated accountability for profits unambiguously to the divisions.

- Encourage higher-level managers to delegate operational decisions.

  Example: At one global charitable organization, country-level managers' inability to delegate led to decision paralysis. So the leader-ship team encouraged country managers to delegate standard operational tasks. This freed these managers to focus on developing the strategies needed to fulfill the organization's mission.

Information Flow

- Make sure important information about the competitive environment flows quickly to corporate headquarters. That way, the top team can identify patterns and promulgate best practices throughout the company.

  Example: At one insurance company, accurate information about projects' viability was censored as it moved up the hierarchy. To improve information

and rewards was weak. This was a company long on micromanaging and second-guessing, and short on accountability. Middle managers spent 40% of their time justifying and reporting upward or questioning the tactical decisions of their direct reports.

Armed with this understanding, the company designed a new management model that established who was accountable for what and made the connection between performance and reward. For instance, the norm at this company, not unusual in the industry, had been to promote people quickly, within 18 months to two years, before they had a chance to see their initiatives through. As a flow to senior levels of management, the company took steps to create a more open, informal culture. Top executives began mingling with unit leaders during management meetings and held regular brown-bag lunches where people discussed the company's most pressing issues.

- Facilitate information flow across organizational boundaries.

  Example: To better manage relationships with large, cross-product customers, a B2B company needed its units to talk with one another. It charged its newly created customer-focused marketing group with encouraging cross-company communication. The group issued regular reports showing performance against targets (by product and geography) and supplied root-cause analyses of performance gaps. Quarterly performance-management meetings further

fostered the trust required for collaboration.

- Help field and line employees understand how their day-to-day choices affect your company's bottom line.

  Example: At a financial services firm, salespeople routinely crafted customized one-off deals with clients that cost the company more than it made in revenues. Sales didn't understand the cost and complexity implications of these transactions. Management addressed the information misalignment by adopting a "smart customization" approach to sales. For customized deals, it established standardized back-office processes (such as risk assessment). It also developed analytical support tools to arm salespeople with accurate information on the cost implications of their proposed transactions. Profitability improved.

result, managers at every level kept doing their old jobs even after they had been promoted, peering over the shoulders of the direct reports who were now in charge of their projects and, all too frequently, taking over. Today, people stay in their positions longer so they can follow through on their own initiatives, and they're still around when the fruits of their labors start to kick in. What's more, results from those initiatives continue to count in their performance reviews for some time after they've been promoted, forcing managers to live with the expectations they'd set in their previous jobs. As a consequence, forecasting has become more accurate and reliable. These actions did yield a structure with fewer layers and greater spans of control, but that was a side effect, not the primary focus, of the changes.

The Elements of Strong Execution

Our conclusions arise out of decades of practical application and intensive research. Nearly five years ago, we and our colleagues set out to gather empirical data to identify the actions that were most effective in enabling an organization to implement strategy. What particular ways of restructuring, motivating, improving information flows, and clarifying decision rights mattered the most? We started by drawing up a list of 17 traits, each corresponding to one or more of the four building blocks we knew could enable effective execution—traits like the free flow of information across organizational boundaries or the degree to which senior leaders refrain from getting involved in operating decisions. With these factors in mind, we developed an online profiler that allows individuals to assess the execution capabilities of their organizations. Over the next four years or so, we collected data from many thousands of profiles, which in turn allowed us to more precisely calibrate the impact of each trait on an organization's ability to execute. That allowed us to rank all 17 traits in order of their relative influence. (See the exhibit "The 17 fundamental traits of organizational effectiveness.)

Ranking the traits makes clear how important decision rights and information are to effective strategy execution. The first eight traits map directly to decision rights and information. Only three of the 17 traits relate to structure, and none of those ranks higher than 13th. We'll walk through the top five traits here.

1. Everyone has a good idea of the decisions and actions for which he or she is responsible

In companies strong on execution, 71% of individuals agree with this statement; that figure drops to 32% in organizations weak on execution.

The 17 fundamental traits of organizational effectiveness

From our survey research drawn from more than 26,000 people in 31 companies, we have distilled the traits that make organizations effective at implementing strategy. Here they are, in order of importance.

Rank		Organization trait	Strength index (out of 100)
1		Everyone has a good idea of the decisions and actions for which he or she is responsible.	81
2		Important information about the competitive environment gets to headquarters quickly.	68
3		Once made, decisions are rarely second-guessed.	58
4		Information flows freely across organizational boundaries.	58
5		Field and line employees usually have the information they need to understand the bottom-line impact of their day-to-day choices.	55
6		Line managers have access to the metrics they need to measure the key drivers of their business.	48
7		Managers up the line get involved in operating decisions.	32
8		Conflicting messages are rarely sent to the market.	32
9		The individual performance-appraisal process differentiates among high, adequate, and low performers.	32
10		The ability to deliver on performance commitments strongly influences career advancement and compensation.	32
11		It is more accurate to describe the culture of this organization as "persuade and cajole" than "command and control."	29
12		The primary role of corporate staff here is to support the business units rather than to audit them.	29
13		Promotions can be lateral moves (from one position to another on the same level in the hierarchy).	29
14		Fast-track employees here can expect promotions more frequently than every three years.	23
15		On average, middle managers here have five or more direct reports.	19
16		If the firm has a bad year, but a particular division has a good year, the division head would still get a bonus.	13
17		Besides pay, many other things motivate individuals to do a good job.	10

Building blocks ■ Decision rights Information ▨ Motivators ▨ Structure

About the Data

WE TESTED ORGANIZATIONAL EFFECTIVENESS by having people fill out an online diagnostic, a tool comprising 19 questions (17 that describe organizational traits and two that describe outcomes).

To determine which of the 17 traits in our profiler are most strongly associated with excellence in execution, we looked at 31 companies in our database for which we had responses from at least 150 individual (anonymously completed) profiles, for a total of 26,743 responses. Applying regression analysis to each of the 31 data sets, we correlated the 17 traits with our measure of organizational effectiveness, which we defined as an affirmative response to the outcome statement, "Important strategic and operational decisions are quickly translated into action." Then we ranked the traits in order, according to the number of data sets in which the trait exhibited a significant correlation with our measure of success within a 90% confidence interval. Finally, we indexed the result to a 100-point scale. The top trait—"Everyone has a good idea of the decisions and actions for which he or she is responsible"—exhibited a significant positive correlation with our success indicator in 25 of the 31 data sets, for an index score of 81.

Blurring of decision rights tends to occur as a company matures. Young organizations are generally too busy getting things done to define roles and responsibilities clearly at the outset. And why should they? In a small company, it's not so difficult to know what other people are up to. So for a time, things work out well enough. As the company grows, however, executives come and go, bringing in with them and taking away different expectations, and over time the approval process gets ever more convoluted and murky. It becomes increasingly unclear where one person's accountability begins and another's ends.

One global consumer-durables company found this out the hard way. It was so rife with people making competing and conflicting decisions that it was hard to find anyone below the CEO who felt truly accountable for profitability. The company was organized into 16 product divisions aggregated into three geographic groups—North America, Europe, and International. Each of the divisions was charged with reaching explicit performance targets, but functional staff at corporate headquarters controlled spending targets—how R&D dollars were allocated, for instance. Decisions made by divisional and geographic leaders were routinely overridden by functional leaders. Overhead costs began to mount as the divisions added staff to help them create bulletproof cases to challenge corporate decisions.

Decisions stalled while divisions negotiated with functions, each layer weighing in with questions. Functional staffers in the divisions (financial analysts, for example) often deferred to their higher-ups in corporate rather than their division vice president, since functional leaders were responsible for rewards and promotions. Only the CEO and his executive team had the discretion to resolve disputes. All of these symptoms fed on one another and collectively hampered execution—until a new CEO came in.

The new chief executive chose to focus less on cost control and more on profitable growth by redefining the divisions to focus on consumers. As part of the new organizational model, the CEO designated accountability for profits unambiguously to the divisions and also gave them the authority to draw on functional activities to support their goals (as well as more control of the budget). Corporate functional roles and decision rights were recast to better support the divisions' needs and also to build the cross-divisional links necessary for developing the global capabilities of the business as a whole. For the most part, the functional leaders understood the market realities—and that change entailed some adjustments to the operating model of the business. It helped that the CEO brought them into the organizational redesign process, so that the new model wasn't something imposed on them as much as it was something they engaged in and built together.

2. Important information about the competitive environment gets to headquarters quickly

On average, 77% of individuals in strong-execution organizations agree with this statement, whereas only 45% of those in weak-execution organizations do.

Headquarters can serve a powerful function in identifying patterns and promulgating best practices throughout business segments and geographic regions. But it can play this coordinating role only if it has accurate and up-to-date market intelligence. Otherwise, it will tend to impose its own agenda and policies rather than defer to operations that are much closer to the customer.

Consider the case of heavy-equipment manufacturer Caterpillar.[1] Today it is a highly successful $45 billion global company, but a generation ago, Caterpillar's organization was so badly misaligned that its very existence was threatened. Decision rights were hoarded at the top by functional general offices located at headquarters in Peoria, Illinois, while much of the information needed to make those decisions resided in the field with sales managers. "It just took a long time to get decisions going up and down the functional silos, and they really weren't good business decisions; they were more functional decisions," noted one field executive. Current CEO Jim Owens, then a managing director in Indonesia, told us that such information that did make it to the top had been "whitewashed and varnished several times over along the way." Cut off from information about the external market, senior executives focused on the organization's internal workings, overanalyzing issues and second-guessing decisions made at lower levels, costing the company opportunities in fast-moving markets.

Pricing, for example, was based on cost and determined not by market realities but by the pricing general office in Peoria. Sales representatives across the world lost sale after sale to Komatsu, whose competitive pricing consistently beat Caterpillar's. In 1982, the company posted the first annual loss in its almost-60-year history. In 1983 and 1984, it lost $1 million a day, seven days a week. By the end of 1984, Caterpillar had lost a billion dollars. By 1988, then-CEO George Schaefer stood atop an entrenched bureaucracy that was, in his words, "telling me what I wanted to hear, not what I needed to know." So, he convened a task force of "renegade" middle managers and tasked them with charting Caterpillar's future.

Ironically, the way to ensure that the right information flowed to headquarters was to make sure the right decisions were made much further down the organization. By delegating operational responsibility to the people closer to the action, top executives were free to focus on more global strategic issues. Accordingly, the company reorganized into business units, making each accountable for its own P&L statement. The functional general offices that had been all-powerful ceased to exist, literally overnight. Their talent and expertise, including engineering, pricing, and manufacturing, were parceled out to the new business units, which could now design their own products, develop their own manufacturing processes and schedules, and set their own prices. The move dramatically decentralized decision rights, giving the units control over market decisions. The business unit P&Ls were now measured consistently across the enterprise, as return on assets became the universal measure of success. With this accurate, up-to-date, and directly comparable information, senior decision makers at headquarters could make smart strategic choices and trade-offs rather than use outdated sales data to make ineffective, tactical marketing decisions.

Within 18 months, the company was working in the new model. "This was a revolution that became a renaissance," Owens recalls, "a spectacular transformation of a kind of sluggish company into one that actually has entrepreneurial zeal. And that transition was very quick because it was decisive and it was complete; it was thorough; it was universal, worldwide, all at one time."

3. Once made, decisions are rarely second-guessed
Whether someone is second-guessing depends on your vantage point. A more senior and broader enterprise perspective can add value to a decision, but managers up the line may not be adding incremental value; instead, they may be stalling progress by redoing their subordinates' jobs while, in effect, shirking their own. In our research, 71% of respondents in weak-execution companies thought that decisions were being second-guessed, whereas only 45% of those from strong-execution organizations felt that way.

Recently, we worked with a global charitable organization dedicated to alleviating poverty. It had a problem others might envy: It was suffering from the strain brought on by a rapid growth in donations and a corresponding increase in the depth and breadth of its program offerings. As you might expect, this nonprofit was populated with people on a mission who took intense personal ownership of projects. It did not reward the delegation of even the most mundane administrative tasks. Country-level managers, for example, would personally oversee copier repairs. Managers' inability to delegate led to decision paralysis and a lack of accountability as the organization grew. Second-guessing was an art form. When there was doubt over who was empowered to make a decision, the default was often to have a series of meetings in which no decision was reached. When decisions were finally made, they had generally been vetted by so many parties that no one person could be held accountable. An effort to expedite decision-making through restructuring—by collocating key leaders with subject-matter experts in newly established central and regional centers of excellence—became instead another logjam. Key managers still weren't sure of their right to take advantage of these centers, so they didn't.

The nonprofit's management and directors went back to the drawing board. We worked with them to design a decision-making map, a tool to help identify where different types of decisions should be taken, and with it they clarified and enhanced decision rights at all levels of management. All managers were then actively encouraged to delegate standard operational tasks. Once people had a clear idea of what decisions they should and should not be making, holding them accountable for decisions felt fair. What's more, now they could focus their energies on the organization's mission. Clarifying decision rights and responsibilities also improved the organization's ability to track individual achievement, which helped it chart new and appealing career-advancement paths.

4. Information flows freely across organizational boundaries
When information does not flow horizontally across different parts of the company, units behave like silos, forfeiting economies of scale and the transfer of best practices. Moreover, the organization as a whole loses the opportunity to develop a cadre of up-and-coming managers well versed in all aspects of the company's operations. Our research indicates that only 21% of respondents from weak-execution companies thought information flowed freely across organizational boundaries whereas 55% of those from strong-execution firms did.

Since scores for even the strong companies are pretty low, though, this is an issue that most companies can work on.

A cautionary tale comes from a business-to-business company whose customer and product teams failed to collaborate in serving a key segment: large, cross-product customers. To manage relationships with important clients, the company had established a customer-focused marketing group, which developed customer outreach programs, innovative pricing models, and tailored promotions and discounts. But this group issued no clear and consistent reports of its initiatives and progress to the product units and had difficulty securing time with the regular cross-unit management to discuss key performance issues. Each product unit communicated and planned in its own way, and it took tremendous energy for the customer group to understand the units' various priorities and tailor communications to each one. So the units were not aware, and had little faith, that this new division was making constructive inroads into a key customer segment. Conversely (and predictably), the customer team felt the units paid only perfunctory attention to its plans and couldn't get their cooperation on issues critical to multiproduct customers, such as potential trade-offs and volume discounts.

Historically, this lack of collaboration hadn't been a problem because the company had been the dominant player in a high-margin market. But as the market became more competitive, customers began to view the firm as unreliable and, generally, as a difficult supplier, and they became increasingly reluctant to enter into favorable relationships.

Once the issues became clear, though, the solution wasn't terribly complicated, involving little more than getting the groups to talk to one another. The customer division became responsible for issuing regular reports to the product units showing performance against targets, by product and geographic region, and for supplying a supporting root-cause analysis. A standing performance-management meeting was placed on the schedule every quarter, creating a forum for exchanging information face-to-face and discussing outstanding issues. These moves bred the broader organizational trust required for collaboration.

5. Field and line employees usually have the information they need to understand the bottom-line impact of their day-to-day choices

Rational decisions are necessarily bounded by the information available to employees. If managers don't understand what it will cost to capture an incremental dollar in revenue, they will always pursue the incremental revenue. They can hardly be faulted, even if their decision is—in the light of full information—wrong. Our research shows that 61% of individuals in strong-execution organizations agree that field and line employees have the information they need to understand the bottom-line impact of their decisions. This figure plummets to 28% in weak-execution organizations.

We saw this unhealthy dynamic play out at a large, diversified financial-services client, which had been built through a series of successful mergers of small regional banks. In combining operations, managers had chosen to separate front-office bankers who sold loans from back-office support groups who did risk assessments, placing each in a different reporting relationship and, in many cases, in different locations. Unfortunately, they failed to institute the necessary information and motivation links to ensure smooth operations. As a result, each pursued different, and often competing, goals.

For example, salespeople would routinely enter into highly customized one-off deals with clients that cost the company more than they made in revenues. Sales did not have a clear understanding of the cost and complexity implications of these transactions. Without sufficient information, sales staff believed that the back-end people were sabotaging their deals, while the support groups considered the front-end people to be cowboys. At year's end, when the data were finally reconciled, management would bemoan the sharp increase in operational costs, which often erased the profit from these transactions.

Executives addressed this information misalignment by adopting a "smart customization" approach to sales. They standardized the end-to-end processes used in the majority of deals and allowed for customization only in select circumstances. For these customized deals, they established clear back-office processes and analytical support tools to arm salespeople with accurate information on the cost implications of the proposed transactions. At the same time, they rolled out common reporting standards and tools for both the front- and back-office operations to ensure that each group had access to the same data and metrics when making decisions. Once each side understood the business realities confronted by the other, they cooperated more effectively, acting in the whole company's best interests—and there were no more year-end surprises.

Creating a Transformation Program

The four building blocks that managers can use to improve strategy execution—decision rights, information, structure, and motivators—are inextricably linked. Unclear decision rights not only paralyze decision making but also impede information flow, divorce performance from rewards, and prompt work-arounds that subvert formal reporting lines. Blocking information results in poor decisions, limited career development, and a reinforcement of structural silos. So what to do about it?

Since each organization is different and faces a unique set of internal and external variables, there is no universal answer to that question. The first step is to identify the sources of the problem. In our work, we often begin by having a company's employees take our profiling survey and consolidating the results. The more people in the organization who take the survey, the better.

Once executives understand their company's areas of weakness, they can take any number of actions. The exhibit, "Mapping improvement tactics to the building blocks" shows 15 possible steps that can have an impact on performance. (The options listed represent only a sampling of the dozens of choices managers might make.) All of these actions are geared toward strengthening one or more of the 17 traits. For example, if you were to take steps to "clarify and streamline decision making" you could potentially strengthen two traits: "Everyone has a good idea of the decisions and actions for which he or she is responsible," and "Once made, decisions are rarely second-guessed."

Mapping improvements to the building blocks: Some sample tactics

Companies can take a host of steps to improve their ability to execute strategy. The 15 here are only some of the possible examples. Every one strengthens one or more of the building blocks executives can use to improve their strategy-execution capability: clarifying decision rights, improving information, establishing the right motivators, and restructuring the organization.

■ Focus corporate staff on supporting business-unit decision making.

■ Clarify and streamline decision making at each operating level.

■ Focus headquarters on important strategic questions.

■ ☐ Create centers of excellence by consolidating similar functions into a single organizational unit.

■ ☐ ▨ Assign process owners to coordinate activities that span organizational functions.

■ ▨ Establish individual performance measures.

☐ Improve field-to-headquarters information flow.

☐ Define and distribute daily operating metrics to the field or line.

☐ ▨ Create cross-functional teams.

▨ Introduce differentiating performance awards.

▨ Expand nonmonetary rewards to recognize exceptional performers.

☐ ▨ Increase position tenure.

☐ ▨ Institute lateral moves and rotations.

▨ Broaden spans of control.

▨ Decrease layers of management.

Building blocks ■ Decision rights ☐ Information ▨ Motivators ▨ Structure

You certainly wouldn't want to put 15 initiatives in a single trans-formation program. Most organizations don't have the managerial capacity or organizational appetite to take on more than five or six at a time. And as we've stressed, you should first take steps to address decision rights and information, and then design the necessary changes to motivators and structure to support the new design.

To help companies understand their shortcomings and construct the improvement program that will have the greatest impact, we have developed an organizational-change simulator. This interac-tive tool accompanies the profiler, allowing you to try out different elements of a change program virtually, to see which ones will best target your company's particular area of weakness. (For an overview of the simulation process, see the sidebar "Test Drive Your Organiza-tion's Transformation.")

To get a sense of the process from beginning to end–from taking the diagnostic profiler, to formulating your strategy, to launching your organizational transformation–consider the experience of a leading insurance company we'll call Goodward Insurance. Good-ward was a successful company with strong capital reserves and steady revenue and customer growth. Still, its leadership wanted to further enhance execution to deliver on an ambitious five-year stra-tegic agenda that included aggressive targets in customer growth, revenue increases, and cost reduction, which would require a new level of teamwork. While there were pockets of cross-unit collabo-ration within the company, it was far more common for each unit to focus on its own goals, making it difficult to spare resources to support another unit's goals. In many cases there was little incen-tive to do so anyway: Unit A's goals might require the involvement of Unit B to succeed, but Unit B's goals might not include supporting Unit A's effort.

The company had initiated a number of enterprisewide proj-ects over the years, which had been completed on time and on budget, but these often had to be reworked because stakeholder needs hadn't been sufficiently taken into account. After launching a shared-services center, for example, the company had to revisit its operating model and processes when units began hiring shadow

Test-Drive Your Organization's Transformation

YOU KNOW YOUR ORGANIZATION could perform better. You are faced with dozens of levers you could conceivably pull if you had unlimited time and resources. But you don't. You operate in the real world.

How, then, do you make the most-educated and cost-efficient decisions about which change initiatives to implement? We've developed a way to test the efficacy of specific actions (such as clarifying decision rights, forming cross-functional teams, or expanding nonmonetary rewards) without risking significant amounts of time and money. You can go to www .simulator-orgeffectiveness.com to assemble and try out various five-step organizational-change programs and assess which would be the most effective and efficient in improving execution at your company.

You begin the simulation by selecting one of seven organizational profiles that most resembles the current state of your organization. If you're not sure, you can take a five-minute diagnostic survey. This online survey automatically generates an organizational profile and baseline execution-effectiveness score. (Although 100 is a perfect score, nobody is perfect; even the most effective companies often score in the 60s and 70s.)

Having established your baseline, you use the simulator to chart a possible course you'd like to take to improve your execution capabilities by selecting five out of a possible 28 actions. Ideally, these moves should directly address the weakest links in your organizational profile. To help you make the right choices, the simulator offers insights that shed further light on how a proposed action influences particular organizational elements.

---

staff to focus on priority work that the center wouldn't expedite. The center might decide what technology applications, for instance, to develop on its own rather than set priorities according to what was most important to the organization.

In a similar way, major product launches were hindered by insufficient coordination among departments. The marketing department would develop new coverage options without asking the claims-processing group whether it had the ability to process the claims. Since it didn't, processors had to create expensive manual workarounds when the new kinds of claims started pouring in. Nor did

Once you have made your selections, the simulator executes the steps you've elected and processes them through a web-based engine that evaluates them using empirical relationships identified from 31 companies representing more than 26,000 data observations. It then generates a bar chart indicating how much your organization's execution score has improved and where it now stands in relation to the highest-performing companies from our research and the scores of other people like you who have used the simulator starting from the same original profile you did. If you wish, you may then advance to the next round and pick another five actions. What you will see is illustrated above.

The beauty of the simulator is its ability to consider—consequence-free—the impact on execution of endless combinations of possible actions. Each simulation includes only two rounds, but you can run the simulation as many times as you like. The simulator has also been used for team competition within organizations, and we've found that it engenders very engaging and productive dialogue among senior executives.

While the simulator cannot capture all of the unique situations an organization might face, it is a useful tool for assessing and building a targeted and effective organization-transformation program. It serves as a vehicle to stimulate thinking about the impact of various changes, saving untold amounts of time and resources in the process.

marketing ask the actuarial department how these products would affect the risk profile and reimbursement expenses of the company, and for some of the new products, costs did indeed increase.

To identify the greatest barriers to building a stronger execution culture, Goodward Insurance gave the diagnostic survey to all of its 7,000-plus employees and compared the organization's scores on the 17 traits with those from strong-execution companies. Numerous previous surveys (employee-satisfaction, among others) had elicited qualitative comments identifying the barriers to execution excellence. But the diagnostic survey gave the company quantifiable data that it could analyze by group and by management level to determine which barriers were most hindering the people actually charged with execution. As it turned out, middle management was far more pessimistic than the top executives in their assessment of the organization's execution ability. Their input became especially critical to the change agenda ultimately adopted.

Through the survey, Goodward Insurance uncovered impediments to execution in three of the most influential organizational traits:

Information did not flow freely across organizational boundaries. Sharing information was never one of Goodward's hallmarks, but managers had always dismissed the mounting anecdotal evidence of poor cross-divisional information flow as "some other group's problem." The organizational diagnostic data, however, exposed such plausible deniability as an inadequate excuse. In fact, when the CEO reviewed the profiler results with his direct reports, he held up the chart on cross-group information flows and declared, "We've been discussing this problem for several years, and yet you always say that it's so-and-so's problem, not mine. Sixty-seven percent of [our] respondents said that they do not think information flows freely across divisions. This is not so-and-so's problem—it's our problem. You just don't get results that low [unless it comes] from everywhere. We are all on the hook for fixing this."

Contributing to this lack of horizontal information flow was a dearth of lateral promotions. Because Goodward had always promoted up rather than over and up, most middle and senior managers remained within a single group. They were not adequately apprised of the activities of the other groups, nor did they have a network of contacts across the organization.

Important information about the competitive environment did not get to headquarters quickly. The diagnostic data and subsequent surveys and interviews with middle management revealed that the wrong information was moving up the org chart. Mundane day-to-day decisions were escalated to the executive level—the top team had to approve midlevel hiring decisions, for instance, and bonuses of $1,000—limiting Goodward's agility in responding to competitors' moves, customers' needs, and changes in the broader marketplace. Meanwhile, more important information was so heavily filtered as it moved up the hierarchy that it was all but worthless for rendering key verdicts. Even if lower-level managers knew that a certain project could never work for highly valid reasons, they would not communicate that dim view to the top team. Nonstarters not only started, they kept going. For instance, the company had a project under way to create new incentives for its brokers. Even though this approach had been previously tried without success, no one spoke up in meetings or stopped the project because it was a priority for one of the top-team members.

No one had a good idea of the decisions and actions for which he or she was responsible. The general lack of information flow extended to decision rights, as few managers understood where their authority ended and another's began. Accountability even for day-to-day decisions was unclear, and managers did not know whom to ask for clarification. Naturally, confusion over decision rights led to second-guessing. Fifty-five percent of respondents felt that decisions were regularly second-guessed at Goodward.

To Goodward's credit, its top executives immediately responded to the results of the diagnostic by launching a change program targeted at all three problem areas. The program integrated early, often symbolic, changes with longer-term initiatives, in an effort to build momentum and galvanize participation and ownership. Recognizing that a passive-aggressive attitude toward people perceived to be in power solely as a result of their position in the hierarchy was hindering information flow, they took immediate steps to signal their intention to create a more informal and open culture. One symbolic change: the seating at management meetings was rearranged. The top executives used to sit in a separate section, the physical space between them and the rest of the room fraught with symbolism. Now they intermingled, making themselves more accessible and encouraging people to share information informally. Regular brown-bag lunches were established with members of the C-suite, where people had a chance to discuss the overall culture-change initiative, decision rights, new mechanisms for communicating across the units, and so forth. Seating at these events was highly choreographed to ensure that a mix of units was represented at each table. Icebreaker activities were designed to encourage individuals to learn about other units' work.

Meanwhile, senior managers commenced the real work of remedying issues relating to information flows and decision rights. They assessed their own informal networks to understand how people making key decisions got their information, and they identified critical gaps. The outcome was a new framework for making important decisions that clearly specifies who owns each decision, who must provide input, who is ultimately accountable for the results, and how results are defined. Other longer-term initiatives include:

- Pushing certain decisions down into the organization to better align decision rights with the best available information. Most hiring and bonus decisions, for instance, have been delegated to immediate managers, so long as they are within preestablished boundaries relating to numbers hired and salary levels. Being clear about who needs what information is encouraging cross-group dialogue.

- Identifying and eliminating duplicative committees.

- Pushing metrics and scorecards down to the group level, so that rather than focus on solving the mystery of *who* caused a problem, management can get right to the root cause of *why* the problem occurred. A well-designed scorecard captures not only outcomes (like sales volume or revenue) but also leading indicators of those outcomes (such as the number of customer calls or completed customer plans). As a result, the focus of management conversations has shifted from trying to explain the past to charting the future—anticipating and preventing problems.

- Making the planning process more inclusive. Groups are explicitly mapping out the ways their initiatives depend on and affect one another; shared group goals are assigned accordingly.

- Enhancing the middle management career path to emphasize the importance of lateral moves to career advancement.

Goodward Insurance has just embarked on this journey. The insurer has distributed ownership of these initiatives among various groups and management levels so that these efforts don't become silos in themselves. Already, solid improvement in the company's execution is beginning to emerge. The early evidence of success has come from employee-satisfaction surveys: Middle management responses to the questions about levels of cross-unit collaboration and clarity of decision making have improved as much as 20 to 25 percentage points. And high performers are already reaching across boundaries to gain a broader understanding of the full business, even if it doesn't mean a better title right away.

Execution is a notorious and perennial challenge. Even at the companies that are best at it—what we call "resilient organizations"—just two-thirds of employees agree that important strategic and operational decisions are quickly translated into action. As long as companies continue to attack their execution problems primarily or solely with structural or motivational initiatives, they will continue to fail. As we've seen, they may enjoy short-term results, but they will inevitably slip back into old habits because they won't have addressed the root causes of failure. Such failures can almost always be fixed by ensuring that people truly understand what they are responsible for and who makes which decisions—and then giving them the information they need to fulfill their responsibilities. With these two building blocks in place, structural and motivational elements will follow.

Originally published in June 2008. Reprint R0806C

Note

1. The details for this example have been taken from Gary L. Neilson and Bruce A. Pasternack, *Results: Keep What's Good, Fix What's Wrong, and Unlock Great Performance* (Random House, 2005).

The Focused Leader

by Daniel Goleman

A PRIMARY TASK OF LEADERSHIP is to direct attention. To do so, leaders must learn to focus their own attention. When we speak about being focused, we commonly mean thinking about one thing while filtering out distractions. But a wealth of recent research in neuroscience shows that we focus in many ways, for different purposes, drawing on different neural pathways—some of which work in concert, while others tend to stand in opposition.

Grouping these modes of attention into three broad buckets—focusing on *yourself,* focusing on *others,* and focusing on *the wider world*—sheds new light on the practice of many essential leadership skills. Focusing inward and focusing constructively on others helps leaders cultivate the primary elements of emotional intelligence. A fuller understanding of how they focus on the wider world can improve their ability to devise strategy, innovate, and manage organizations.

Every leader needs to cultivate this triad of awareness, in abundance and in the proper balance, because a failure to focus inward leaves you rudderless, a failure to focus on others renders you clueless, and a failure to focus outward may leave you blindsided.

Focusing On Yourself

Emotional intelligence begins with self-awareness—getting in touch with your inner voice. Leaders who heed their inner voices can draw on more resources to make better decisions and connect with their authentic selves. But what does that entail? A look at how people focus inward can make this abstract concept more concrete.

Self-awareness

Hearing your inner voice is a matter of paying careful attention to internal physiological signals. These subtle cues are monitored by the insula, which is tucked behind the frontal lobes of the brain. Attention given to any part of the body amps up the insula's sensitivity to that part. Tune in to your heartbeat, and the insula activates more neurons in that circuitry. How well people can sense their heartbeats has, in fact, become a standard way to measure their self-awareness.

Gut feelings are messages from the insula and the amygdala, which the neuroscientist Antonio Damasio, of the University of Southern California, calls *somatic markers*. Those messages are sensations that something "feels" right or wrong. Somatic markers simplify decision making by guiding our attention toward better options. They're hardly foolproof (how often was that feeling that you left the stove on correct?), so the more comprehensively we read them, the better we use our intuition. (See "Are You Skimming This Sidebar?")

Consider, for example, the implications of an analysis of interviews conducted by a group of British researchers with 118 professional traders and 10 senior managers at four City of London investment banks. The most successful traders (whose annual income averaged £500,000) were neither the ones who relied entirely on analytics nor the ones who just went with their guts. They focused on a full range of emotions, which they used to judge the value of their intuition. When they suffered losses, they acknowledged their anxiety, became more cautious, and took fewer risks. The least successful traders (whose income averaged only £100,000) tended to ignore their anxiety and keep going with their guts. Because they failed to heed a wider array of internal signals, they were misled.

Zeroing in on sensory impressions of ourselves in the moment is one major element of self-awareness. But another is critical to leadership: combining our experiences across time into a coherent view of our authentic selves.

Idea in Brief

The Problem

A primary task of leadership is to direct attention. To do so, leaders must learn to focus their own attention.

The Argument

People commonly think of "being focused" as filtering out distractions while concentrating on one thing. But a wealth of recent neuroscience research shows that we focus attention in many ways, for different purposes, while drawing on different neural pathways.

The Solution

Every leader needs to cultivate a triad of awareness—an inward focus, a focus on others, and an outward focus. Focusing inward and focusing on others helps leaders cultivate emotional intelligence. Focusing outward can improve their ability to devise strategy, innovate, and manage organizations.

To be authentic is to be the same person to others as you are to yourself. In part that entails paying attention to what others think of you, particularly people whose opinions you esteem and who will be candid in their feedback. A variety of focus that is useful here is *open awareness,* in which we broadly notice what's going on around us without getting caught up in or swept away by any particular thing. In this mode we don't judge, censor, or tune out; we simply perceive.

Leaders who are more accustomed to giving input than to receiving it may find this tricky. Someone who has trouble sustaining open awareness typically gets snagged by irritating details, such as fellow travelers in the airport security line who take forever getting their carry-ons into the scanner. Someone who can keep her attention in open mode will notice the travelers but not worry about them, and will take in more of her surroundings. (See the sidebar "Expand Your Awareness.")

Of course, being open to input doesn't guarantee that someone will provide it. Sadly, life affords us few chances to learn how others really see us, and even fewer for executives as they rise through the ranks. That may be why one of the most popular and overenrolled courses at Harvard Business School is Bill George's Authentic Leadership Development, in which George has created what he calls True North groups to heighten this aspect of self-awareness.

Are You Skimming This Sidebar?

DO YOU HAVE TROUBLE remembering what someone has just told you in conversation? Did you drive to work this morning on autopilot? Do you focus more on your smartphone than on the person you're having lunch with?

Attention is a mental muscle; like any other muscle, it can be strengthened through the right kind of exercise. The fundamental rep for building deliberate attention is simple: When your mind wanders, notice that it has wandered, bring it back to your desired point of focus, and keep it there as long as you can. That basic exercise is at the root of virtually every kind of meditation. Meditation builds concentration and calmness and facilitates recovery from the agitation of stress.

So does a video game called Tenacity, now in development by a design group and neuroscientists at the University of Wisconsin. Slated for release in 2014, the game offers a leisurely journey through any of half a dozen scenes, from a barren desert to a fantasy staircase spiraling heavenward. At the beginner's level you tap an iPad screen with one finger every time you exhale; the challenge is to tap two fingers with every fifth breath. As you move to higher levels, you're presented with more distractions—a helicopter flies into view, a plane does a flip, a flock of birds suddenly scud by.

When players are attuned to the rhythm of their breathing, they experience the strengthening of selective attention as a feeling of calm focus, as in meditation. Stanford University is exploring that connection at its Calming Technology Lab, which is developing relaxing devices, such as a belt that detects your breathing rate. Should a chock-full in-box, for instance, trigger what has been called e-mail apnea, an iPhone app can guide you through exercises to calm your breathing and your mind.

These groups (which anyone can form) are based on the precept that self-knowledge begins with self-revelation. Accordingly, they are open and intimate, "a safe place," George explains, "where members can discuss personal issues they do not feel they can raise elsewhere—often not even with their closest family members." What good does that do? "We don't know who we are until we hear ourselves speaking the story of our lives to those we trust," George says. It's a structured way to match our view of our true selves with the views our most trusted colleagues have—an external check on our authenticity.

Expand Your Awareness

JUST AS A CAMERA LENS can be set narrowly on a single point or more widely to take in a panoramic view, you can focus tightly or expansively.

One measure of open awareness presents people with a stream of letters and numbers, such as S, K, O, E, 4, R, T, 2, H, P. In scanning the stream, many people will notice the first number, 4, but after that their attention blinks. Those firmly in open awareness mode will register the second number as well.

Strengthening the ability to maintain open awareness requires leaders to do something that verges on the unnatural: cultivate at least sometimes a willingness to not be in control, not offer up their own views, not judge others. That's less a matter of deliberate action than of attitude adjustment.

One path to making that adjustment is through the classic power of positive thinking, because pessimism narrows our focus, whereas positive emotions widen our attention and our receptiveness to the new and unexpected. A simple way to shift into positive mode is to ask yourself, "If everything worked out perfectly in my life, what would I be doing in 10 years?" Why is that effective? Because when you're in an upbeat mood, the University of Wisconsin neuroscientist Richard Davidson has found, your brain's left prefrontal area lights up. That area harbors the circuitry that reminds us how great we'll feel when we reach some long-sought goal.

"Talking about positive goals and dreams activates brain centers that open you up to new possibilities," says Richard Boyatzis, a psychologist at Case Western Reserve. "But if you change the conversation to what you should do to fix yourself, it closes you down. . . . You need the negative to survive, but the positive to thrive."

Self-control

"Cognitive control" is the scientific term for putting one's attention where one wants it and keeping it there in the face of temptation to wander. This focus is one aspect of the brain's executive function, which is located in the prefrontal cortex. A colloquial term for it is "willpower."

Cognitive control enables executives to pursue a goal despite distractions and setbacks. The same neural circuitry that allows such a single-minded pursuit of goals also manages unruly emotions. Good cognitive control can be seen in people who stay calm in a crisis, tame their own agitation, and recover from a debacle or defeat.

Decades' worth of research demonstrates the singular importance of willpower to leadership success. Particularly compelling is a longitudinal study tracking the fates of all 1,037 children born during a single year in the 1970s in the New Zealand city of Dunedin. For several years during childhood the children were given a battery of tests of willpower, including the psychologist Walter Mischel's legendary "marshmallow test"—a choice between eating one marshmallow right away and getting two by waiting 15 minutes. In Mischel's experiments, roughly a third of children grab the marshmallow on the spot, another third hold out for a while longer, and a third manage to make it through the entire quarter hour.

Years later, when the children in the Dunedin study were in their 30s and all but 4% of them had been tracked down again, the researchers found that those who'd had the cognitive control to resist the marshmallow longest were significantly healthier, more successful financially, and more law-abiding than the ones who'd been unable to hold out at all. In fact, statistical analysis showed that a child's level of self-control was a more powerful predictor of financial success than IQ, social class, or family circumstance.

How we focus holds the key to exercising willpower, Mischel says. Three subvarieties of cognitive control are at play when you pit self-restraint against self-gratification: the ability to voluntarily disengage your focus from an object of desire; the ability to resist distraction so that you don't gravitate back to that object; and the ability to concentrate on the future goal and imagine how good you will feel when you achieve it. As adults the children of Dunedin may have been held hostage to their younger selves, but they need not have been, because the power to focus can be developed. (See the sidebar "Learning Self-Restraint.")

Focusing on Others

The word "attention" comes from the Latin *attendere,* meaning "to reach toward." This is a perfect definition of focus on others, which is the foundation of empathy and of an ability to build social relationships—the second and third pillars of emotional intelligence.

Learning Self-Restraint

QUICK, NOW. HERE'S A TEST of cognitive control. In what direction is the middle arrow in each row pointing?

→ → → ← ←
→ ← ← ← ←
→ → ← → →

The test, called the Eriksen Flanker Task, gauges your susceptibility to distraction. When it's taken under laboratory conditions, differences of a thousandth of a second can be detected in the speed with which subjects perceive which direction the middle arrows are pointing. The stronger their cognitive control, the less susceptible they are to distraction.

Interventions to strengthen cognitive control can be as unsophisticated as a game of Simon Says or Red Light—any exercise in which you are asked to stop on cue. Research suggests that the better a child gets at playing Musical Chairs, the stronger his or her prefrontal wiring for cognitive control will become.

Operating on a similarly simple principle is a social and emotional learning (SEL) method that's used to strengthen cognitive control in schoolchildren across the United States. When confronted by an upsetting problem, the children are told to think of a traffic signal. The red light means stop, calm down, and think before you act. The yellow light means slow down and think of several possible solutions. The green light means try out a plan and see how it works. Thinking in these terms allows the children to shift away from amygdala-driven impulses to prefrontal-driven deliberate behavior.

It's never too late for adults to strengthen these circuits as well. Daily sessions of mindfulness practice work in a way similar to Musical Chairs and SEL. In these sessions you focus your attention on your breathing and practice tracking your thoughts and feelings without getting swept away by them. Whenever you notice that your mind has wandered, you simply return it to your breath. It sounds easy—but try it for 10 minutes, and you'll find there's a learning curve.

Executives who can effectively focus on others are easy to recognize. They are the ones who find common ground, whose opinions carry the most weight, and with whom other people want to work. They emerge as natural leaders regardless of organizational or social rank.

The empathy triad

We talk about empathy most commonly as a single attribute. But a close look at where leaders are focusing when they exhibit it reveals three distinct kinds, each important for leadership effectiveness:

- *cognitive empathy*—the ability to understand another person's perspective;

- *emotional empathy*—the ability to feel what someone else feels;

- *empathic concern*—the ability to sense what another person needs from you.

Cognitive empathy enables leaders to explain themselves in meaningful ways—a skill essential to getting the best performance from their direct reports. Contrary to what you might expect, exercising cognitive empathy requires leaders to think about feelings rather than to feel them directly.

An inquisitive nature feeds cognitive empathy. As one successful executive with this trait puts it, "I've always just wanted to learn everything, to understand anybody that I was around—why they thought what they did, why they did what they did, what worked for them, and what didn't work." But cognitive empathy is also an outgrowth of self-awareness. The executive circuits that allow us to think about our own thoughts and to monitor the feelings that flow from them let us apply the same reasoning to other people's minds when we choose to direct our attention that way.

Emotional empathy is important for effective mentoring, managing clients, and reading group dynamics. It springs from ancient parts of the brain beneath the cortex—the amygdala, the hypothalamus, the hippocampus, and the orbitofrontal cortex—that allow us to feel fast without thinking deeply. They tune us in by arousing in our bodies the emotional states of others: I literally feel your pain. My brain patterns match up with yours when I listen to you tell a gripping story. As Tania Singer, the director of the social neuroscience department at the Max Planck Institute for Human Cognitive and Brain Sciences, in Leipzig, says, "You need to understand your own feelings to understand the feelings of others." Accessing your capacity for emotional empathy depends on combining two kinds of attention: a deliberate focus on your own echoes of someone else's

When Empathy Needs to Be Learned

EMOTIONAL EMPATHY CAN BE DEVELOPED. That's the conclusion suggested by research conducted with physicians by Helen Riess, the director of the Empathy and Relational Science Program at Boston's Massachusetts General Hospital. To help the physicians monitor themselves, she set up a program in which they learned to focus using deep, diaphragmatic breathing and to cultivate a certain detachment—to watch an interaction from the ceiling, as it were, rather than being lost in their own thoughts and feelings. "Suspending your own involvement to observe what's going on gives you a mindful awareness of the interaction without being completely reactive," says Riess. "You can see if your own physiology is charged up or balanced. You can notice what's transpiring in the situation." If a doctor realizes that she's feeling irritated, for instance, that may be a signal that the patient is bothered too.

Those who are utterly at a loss may be able to prime emotional empathy essentially by faking it until they make it, Riess adds. If you act in a caring way— looking people in the eye and paying attention to their expressions, even when you don't particularly want to—you may start to feel more engaged.

feelings and an open awareness of that person's face, voice, and other external signs of emotion. (See the sidebar "When Empathy Needs to Be Learned.")

Empathic concern, which is closely related to emotional empathy, enables you to sense not just how people feel but what they need from you. It's what you want in your doctor, your spouse—and your boss. Empathic concern has its roots in the circuitry that compels parents' attention to their children. Watch where people's eyes go when someone brings an adorable baby into a room, and you'll see this mammalian brain center leaping into action.

One neural theory holds that the response is triggered in the amygdala by the brain's radar for sensing danger and in the prefrontal cortex by the release of oxytocin, the chemical for caring. This implies that empathic concern is a double-edged feeling. We intuitively experience the distress of another as our own. But in deciding whether we will meet that person's needs, we deliberately weigh how much we value his or her well-being.

Getting this intuition-deliberation mix right has great implications. Those whose sympathetic feelings become too strong may themselves suffer. In the helping professions, this can lead to

When Empathy Needs to Be Controlled

GETTING A GRIP on our impulse to empathize with other people's feelings can help us make better decisions when someone's emotional flood threatens to overwhelm us.

Ordinarily, when we see someone pricked with a pin, our brains emit a signal indicating that our own pain centers are echoing that distress. But physicians learn in medical school to block even such automatic responses. Their attentional anesthetic seems to be deployed by the temporal-parietal junction and regions of the prefrontal cortex, a circuit that boosts concentration by tuning out emotions. That's what is happening in your brain when you distance yourself from others in order to stay calm and help them. The same neural network kicks in when we see a problem in an emotionally overheated environment and need to focus on looking for a solution. If you're talking with someone who is upset, this system helps you understand the person's perspective intellectually by shifting from the heart-to-heart of emotional empathy to the head-to-heart of cognitive empathy.

---

compassion fatigue; in executives, it can create distracting feelings of anxiety about people and circumstances that are beyond anyone's control. But those who protect themselves by deadening their feelings may lose touch with empathy. Empathic concern requires us to manage our personal distress without numbing ourselves to the pain of others. (See the sidebar "When Empathy Needs to Be Controlled.")

What's more, some lab research suggests that the appropriate application of empathic concern is critical to making moral judgments. Brain scans have revealed that when volunteers listened to tales of people subjected to physical pain, their own brain centers for experiencing such pain lit up instantly. But if the story was about psychological suffering, the higher brain centers involved in empathic concern and compassion took longer to activate. Some time is needed to grasp the psychological and moral dimensions of a situation. The more distracted we are, the less we can cultivate the subtler forms of empathy and compassion.

Building relationships
People who lack social sensitivity are easy to spot—at least for other people. They are the clueless among us. The CFO who is technically

competent but bullies some people, freezes out others, and plays favorites—but when you point out what he has just done, shifts the blame, gets angry, or thinks that you're the problem—is not trying to be a jerk; he's utterly unaware of his shortcomings.

Social sensitivity appears to be related to cognitive empathy. Cognitively empathic executives do better at overseas assignments, for instance, presumably because they quickly pick up implicit norms and learn the unique mental models of a new culture. Attention to social context lets us act with skill no matter what the situation, instinctively follow the universal algorithm for etiquette, and behave in ways that put others at ease. (In another age this might have been called good manners.)

Circuitry that converges on the anterior hippocampus reads social context and leads us intuitively to act differently with, say, our college buddies than with our families or our colleagues. In concert with the deliberative prefrontal cortex, it squelches the impulse to do something inappropriate. Accordingly, one brain test for sensitivity to context assesses the function of the hippocampus. The University of Wisconsin neuroscientist Richard Davidson hypothesizes that people who are most alert to social situations exhibit stronger activity and more connections between the hippocampus and the prefrontal cortex than those who just can't seem to get it right.

The same circuits may be at play when we map social networks in a group—a skill that lets us navigate the relationships in those networks well. People who excel at organizational influence can not only sense the flow of personal connections but also name the people whose opinions hold most sway, and so focus on persuading those who will persuade others.

Alarmingly, research suggests that as people rise through the ranks and gain power, their ability to perceive and maintain personal connections tends to suffer a sort of psychic attrition. In studying encounters between people of varying status, Dacher Keltner, a psychologist at Berkeley, has found that higher-ranking individuals consistently focus their gaze less on lower-ranking people and are more likely to interrupt or to monopolize the conversation.

In fact, mapping attention to power in an organization gives a clear indication of hierarchy: The longer it takes Person A to respond to Person B, the more relative power Person A has. Map response times across an entire organization, and you'll get a remarkably accurate chart of social standing. The boss leaves e-mails unanswered for hours; those lower down respond within minutes. This is so predictable that an algorithm for it—called automated social hierarchy detection—has been developed at Columbia University. Intelligence agencies reportedly are applying the algorithm to suspected terrorist gangs to piece together chains of influence and identify central figures.

But the real point is this: Where we see ourselves on the social ladder sets the default for how much attention we pay. This should be a warning to top executives, who need to respond to fast-moving competitive situations by tapping the full range of ideas and talents within an organization. Without a deliberate shift in attention, their natural inclination may be to ignore smart ideas from the lower ranks.

Focusing on the Wider World

Leaders with a strong outward focus are not only good listeners but also good questioners. They are visionaries who can sense the far-flung consequences of local decisions and imagine how the choices they make today will play out in the future. They are open to the surprising ways in which seemingly unrelated data can inform their central interests. Melinda Gates offered up a cogent example when she remarked on *60 Minutes* that her husband was the kind of person who would read an entire book about fertilizer. Charlie Rose asked, Why fertilizer? The connection was obvious to Bill Gates, who is constantly looking for technological advances that can save lives on a massive scale. "A few billion people would have to die if we hadn't come up with fertilizer," he replied.

Focusing on strategy

Any business school course on strategy will give you the two main elements: exploitation of your current advantage and exploration for new ones. Brain scans that were performed on 63 seasoned business decision makers as they pursued or switched between exploitative and exploratory strategies revealed the specific circuits involved. Not surprisingly, exploitation requires concentration on the job at hand, whereas exploration demands open awareness to recognize new possibilities. But exploitation is accompanied by activity in the brain's circuitry for anticipation and reward. In other words, it feels good to coast along in a familiar routine. When we switch to exploration, we have to make a deliberate cognitive effort to disengage from that routine in order to roam widely and pursue fresh paths.

What keeps us from making that effort? Sleep deprivation, drinking, stress, and mental overload all interfere with the executive circuitry used to make the cognitive switch. To sustain the outward focus that leads to innovation, we need some uninterrupted time in which to reflect and refresh our focus.

The wellsprings of innovation

In an era when almost everyone has access to the same information, new value arises from putting ideas together in novel ways and asking smart questions that open up untapped potential. Moments before we have a creative insight, the brain shows a third-of-a-second spike in gamma waves, indicating the synchrony of far-flung brain cells. The more neurons firing in sync, the bigger the spike. Its timing suggests that what's happening is the formation of a new neural network—presumably creating a fresh association.

But it would be making too much of this to see gamma waves as a secret to creativity. A classic model of creativity suggests how the various modes of attention play key roles. First we prepare our minds by gathering a wide variety of pertinent information, and then we alternate between concentrating intently on the problem and letting our minds wander freely. Those activities translate roughly into vigilance, when while immersing ourselves in all kinds of input, we remain alert for anything relevant to the problem at hand; selective attention to the specific creative challenge; and open awareness, in which we allow our minds to associate freely and the solution to emerge spontaneously. (That's why so many fresh ideas come to people in the shower or out for a walk or a run.)

The dubious gift of systems awareness

If people are given a quick view of a photo of lots of dots and asked to guess how many there are, the strong systems thinkers in the group tend to make the best estimates. This skill shows up in those who are good at designing software, assembly lines, matrix organizations, or interventions to save failing ecosystems—it's a very powerful gift indeed. After all, we live within extremely complex systems. But, suggests the Cambridge University psychologist Simon Baron-Cohen (a cousin of Sacha's), in a small but significant number of people, a strong systems awareness is coupled with an empathy deficit—a blind spot for what other people are thinking and feeling and for reading social situations. For that reason, although people with a superior systems understanding are organizational assets, they are not necessarily effective leaders.

An executive at one bank explained to me that it has created a separate career ladder for systems analysts so that they can progress in status and salary on the basis of their systems smarts alone. That way, the bank can consult them as needed while recruiting leaders from a different pool—one containing people with emotional intelligence.

Putting It All Together

For those who don't want to end up similarly compartmentalized, the message is clear. A focused leader is not the person concentrating on the three most important priorities of the year, or the most brilliant systems thinker, or the one most in tune with the corporate culture. Focused leaders can command the full range of their own attention: They are in touch with their inner feelings, they can control their impulses, they are aware of how others see them, they understand what others need from them, they can weed out distractions and also allow their minds to roam widely, free of preconceptions.

This is challenging. But if great leadership were a paint-by-numbers exercise, great leaders would be more common. Practically every form of focus can be strengthened. What it takes is not talent so much as diligence—a willingness to exercise the attention circuits of the brain just as we exercise our analytic skills and other systems of the body.

The link between attention and excellence remains hidden most of the time. Yet attention is the basis of the most essential of leadership skills—emotional, organizational, and strategic intelligence. And never has it been under greater assault. The constant onslaught of incoming data leads to sloppy shortcuts—triaging our e-mail by reading only the subject lines, skipping many of our voice mails, skimming memos and reports. Not only do our habits of attention make us less effective, but the sheer volume of all those messages leaves us too little time to reflect on what they really mean. This was foreseen more than 40 years ago by the Nobel Prize–winning economist Herbert Simon. Information "consumes the attention of its recipients," he wrote in 1971. "Hence a wealth of information creates a poverty of attention."

My goal here is to place attention center stage so that you can direct it where you need it when you need it. Learn to master your attention, and you will be in command of where you, and your organization, focus.

Originally published in December 2013. Reprint R1312B

Managing Risks

A New Framework. *by Robert S. Kaplan and Anette Mikes*

WHEN TONY HAYWARD BECAME CEO OF BP, in 2007, he vowed to make safety his top priority. Among the new rules he instituted were the requirements that all employees use lids on coffee cups while walking and refrain from texting while driving. Three years later, on Hayward's watch, the *Deepwater Horizon* oil rig exploded in the Gulf of Mexico, causing one of the worst man-made disasters in history. A U.S. investigation commission attributed the disaster to management failures that crippled "the ability of individuals involved to identify the risks they faced and to properly evaluate, communicate, and address them."

Hayward's story reflects a common problem. Despite all the rhetoric and money invested in it, risk management is too often treated as a compliance issue that can be solved by drawing up lots of rules and making sure that all employees follow them. Many such rules, of course, are sensible and do reduce some risks that could severely damage a company. But rules-based risk management will not diminish either the likelihood or the impact of a disaster such as Deepwater Horizon, just as it did not prevent the failure of many financial institutions during the 2007–2008 credit crisis.

Understanding the three categories of risk

The risks that companies face fall into three categories, each of which requires a different risk-management approach. Preventable risks, arising from within an organization, are monitored and controlled through rules, values, and standard compliance tools. In contrast, strategy risks and external risks require distinct processes that encourage managers to openly discuss risks and find cost-effective ways to reduce the likelihood of risk events or mitigate their consequences.

Category 1: Preventable risks	Category 2: Strategy risks	Category 3: External risks
Risks arising from within the company that generate no strategic benefits	Risks taken for superior strategic returns	External, uncontrollable risks
Risk mitigation objective		
Avoid or eliminate occurrence cost-effectively	Reduce likelihood and impact cost-effectively	Reduce impact cost-effectively should risk event occur
Control model		
Integrated culture-and-compliance model: Develop mission statement; values and belief systems; rules and boundary systems; standard operating procedures; internal controls and internal audit	Interactive discussions about risks to strategic objectives drawing on tools such as: • Maps of likelihood and impact of identified risks • Key risk indicator (KRI) scorecards Resource allocation to mitigate critical risk events	"Envisioning" risks through: • Tail-risk assessments and stress testing • Scenario planning • War-gaming
Role of risk-management staff function		
Coordinates, oversees, and revises specific risk controls with internal audit function	Runs risk workshops and risk review meetings Helps develop portfolio of risk initiatives and their funding Acts as devil's advocates	Runs stress-testing, scenario-planning, and war-gaming exercises with management team Acts as devil's advocates
Relationship of the risk-management function to business units		
Acts as independent overseers	Acts as independent facilitators, independent experts, or embedded experts	Complements strategy team or serves as independent facilitators of "envisioning" exercises

Idea in Brief

For all the rhetoric about its importance and the money invested in it, risk management is too often treated as a compliance issue.

A rules-based risk-management system may work well to align values and control employee behavior, but it is unsuitable for managing risks inherent in a company's strategic choices or the risks posed by major disruptions or changes in the external environment. Those types of risk require systems aimed at generating discussion and debate.

For strategy risks, companies must tailor approaches to the scope of the risks involved and their rate of change. Though the risk-management functions may vary from company to company, all such efforts must be anchored in corporate strategic-planning processes.

To manage major external risks outside the company's control, companies can call on tools such as war-gaming and scenario analysis. The choice of approach depends on the immediacy of the potential risk's impact and whether it arises from geopolitical, environmental, economic, or competitive changes.

In this article, we present a new categorization of risk that allows executives to tell which risks can be managed through a rules-based model and which require alternative approaches. We examine the individual and organizational challenges inherent in generating open, constructive discussions about managing the risks related to strategic choices and argue that companies need to anchor these discussions in their strategy formulation and implementation processes. We conclude by looking at how organizations can identify and prepare for nonpreventable risks that arise externally to their strategy and operations.

Managing Risk: Rules or Dialogue?

The first step in creating an effective risk-management system is to understand the qualitative distinctions among the types of risks that organizations face. Our field research shows that risks fall into one of three categories. Risk events from any category can be fatal to a company's strategy and even to its survival.

Identifying and Managing Preventable Risks

COMPANIES CANNOT ANTICIPATE EVERY CIRCUMSTANCE or conflict of interest that an employee might encounter.

Thus, the first line of defense against preventable risk events is to provide guidelines clarifying the company's goals and values.

The Mission

A well-crafted mission statement articulates the organization's fundamental purpose, serving as a "true north" for all employees to follow. The first sentence of Johnson & Johnson's renowned credo, for instance, states, "We believe our first responsibility is to the doctors, nurses and patients, to mothers and fathers, and all others who use our products and services," making clear to all employees whose interests should take precedence in any situation. Mission statements should be communicated to and understood by all employees.

The Values

Companies should articulate the values that guide employee behavior toward principal stakeholders, including customers, suppliers, fellow employees, communities, and shareholders. Clear value statements help employees avoid violating the company's standards and putting its reputation and assets at risk.

Category I: Preventable risks

These are internal risks, arising from within the organization, that are controllable and ought to be eliminated or avoided. Examples are the risks from employees' and managers' unauthorized, illegal, unethical, incorrect, or inappropriate actions and the risks from breakdowns in routine operational processes. To be sure, companies should have a zone of tolerance for defects or errors that would not cause severe damage to the enterprise and for which achieving complete avoidance would be too costly. But in general, companies should seek to eliminate these risks since they get no strategic benefits from taking them on. A rogue trader or an employee bribing a local official may produce some short-term profits for the firm, but over time such actions will diminish the company's value.

The Boundaries

A strong corporate culture clarifies what is not allowed. An explicit definition of boundaries is an effective way to control actions. Consider that
nine of the Ten Commandments and nine of the first 10 amendments to
the U.S. Constitution (commonly known as the Bill of Rights) are written in negative terms. Companies need corporate codes of business conduct that prescribe behaviors relating to conflicts of interest, antitrust issues, trade secrets
and confidential information, bribery, discrimination, and harassment.

Of course, clearly articulated statements of mission, values, and
boundaries don't in themselves ensure good behavior. To counter the
day-to-day pressures of organizational life, top managers must serve
as role models and demonstrate that they mean what they say. Companies must institute strong internal control systems, such as the segre-
gation of duties and an active whistle-blowing program, to reduce not
only misbehavior but also temptation. A capable and independent internal audit department tasked with continually checking employees'
compliance with internal controls and standard operating processes also
will deter employees from violating company procedures and policies and
can detect violations when they do occur.

This risk category is best managed through active prevention:
monitoring operational processes and guiding people's behaviors and
decisions toward desired norms. Since considerable literature already
exists on the rules-based compliance approach, we refer interested
readers to the sidebar "Identifying and Managing Preventable Risks"
in lieu of a full discussion of best practices here.

Category II: Strategy risks

A company voluntarily accepts some risk in order to generate superior returns from its strategy. A bank assumes credit risk, for
example, when it lends money; many companies take on risks
through their research and development activities.

Strategy risks are quite different from preventable risks because
they are not inherently undesirable. A strategy with high expected

returns generally requires the company to take on significant risks, and managing those risks is a key driver in capturing the potential gains. BP accepted the high risks of drilling several miles below the surface of the Gulf of Mexico because of the high value of the oil and gas it hoped to extract.

Strategy risks cannot be managed through a rules-based control model. Instead, you need a risk-management system designed to reduce the probability that the assumed risks actually materialize and to improve the company's ability to manage or contain the risk events should they occur. Such a system would not stop companies from undertaking risky ventures; to the contrary, it would enable companies to take on higher-risk, higher-reward ventures than could competitors with less effec-tive risk management.

Category III: External risks

Some risks arise from events outside the company and are beyond its influence or control. Sources of these risks include natural and political disasters and major macroeconomic shifts. External risks require yet another approach. Because companies cannot prevent such events from occurring, their management must focus on iden-tification (they tend to be obvious in hindsight) and mitigation of their impact.

Companies should tailor their risk-management processes to these different categories. While a compliance-based approach is effective for managing preventable risks, it is wholly inadequate for strategy risks or external risks, which require a fundamentally different approach based on open and explicit risk discussions. That, however, is easier said than done; extensive behavioral and organizational research has shown that individuals have strong cognitive biases that discourage them from thinking about and discussing risk until it's too late.

Why Risk Is Hard to Talk About

Multiple studies have found that people overestimate their ability to influence events that, in fact, are heavily determined by chance. We tend to be *overconfident* about the accuracy of our forecasts and risk assessments and far too narrow in our assessment of the range of outcomes that may occur.

We also *anchor our estimates* to readily available evidence despite the known danger of making linear extrapolations from recent history to a highly uncertain and variable future. We often compound this problem with a *confirmation bias,* which drives us to favor information that supports our positions (typically successes) and suppress information that contradicts them (typically failures). When events depart from our expectations, we tend to *escalate commitment,* irrationally directing even more resources to our failed course of action—throwing good money after bad.

Organizational biases also inhibit our ability to discuss risk and failure. In particular, teams facing uncertain conditions often engage in *groupthink*: Once a course of action has gathered support within a group, those not yet on board tend to suppress their objections—however valid—and fall in line. Groupthink is especially likely if the team is led by an overbearing or overconfident manager who wants to minimize conflict, delay, and challenges to his or her authority.

Collectively, these individual and organizational biases explain why so many companies overlook or misread ambiguous threats. Rather than mitigating risk, firms actually incubate risk through the *normalization of deviance,* as they learn to tolerate apparently minor failures and defects and treat early warning signals as false alarms rather than alerts to imminent danger.

Effective risk-management processes must counteract those biases. "Risk mitigation is painful, not a natural act for humans to perform," says Gentry Lee, the chief systems engineer at Jet Propulsion Laboratory (JPL), a division of the U.S. National Aeronautics and Space Administration. The rocket scientists on JPL project teams are top graduates from elite universities, many of whom have never experienced failure at school or work. Lee's biggest challenge in establishing a new risk culture at JPL was to get project teams to feel comfortable thinking and talking about what could go wrong with their excellent designs.

Rules about what to do and what not to do won't help here. In fact, they usually have the opposite effect, encouraging a checklist mentality that inhibits challenge and discussion. Managing strategy risks and external risks requires very different approaches. We start by examining how to identify and mitigate strategy risks.

Managing Strategy Risks

Over the past 10 years of study, we've come across three distinct approaches to managing strategy risks. Which model is appropriate for a given firm depends largely on the context in which an organization operates. Each approach requires quite different structures and roles for a risk-management function, but all three encourage employees to challenge existing assumptions and debate risk information. Our finding that "one size does not fit all" runs counter to the efforts of regulatory authorities and professional associations to standardize the function.

Independent experts

Some organizations—particularly those like JPL that push the envelope of technological innovation—face high intrinsic risk as they pursue long, complex, and expensive product-development projects. But since much of the risk arises from coping with known laws of nature, the risk changes slowly over time. For these organizations, risk management can be handled at the project level.

JPL, for example, has established a risk review board made up of independent technical experts whose role is to challenge project engineers' design, risk-assessment, and risk-mitigation decisions. The experts ensure that evaluations of risk take place periodically throughout the product-development cycle. Because the risks are relatively unchanging, the review board needs to meet only once or twice a year, with the project leader and the head of the review board meeting quarterly.

The risk review board meetings are intense, creating what Gentry Lee calls "a culture of intellectual confrontation." As board member Chris Lewicki says, "We tear each other apart, throwing stones and giving very critical commentary about everything that's going on." In the process, project engineers see their work from another perspective. "It lifts their noses away from the grindstone," Lewicki adds.

The meetings, both constructive and confrontational, are not intended to inhibit the project team from pursuing highly ambitious missions and designs. But they force engineers to think in advance about how they will describe and defend their design decisions and whether they have sufficiently considered likely failures and defects. The board members, acting as devil's advocates, counterbalance the engineers' natural overconfidence, helping to avoid escalation of commitment to projects with unacceptable levels of risk.

At JPL, the risk review board not only promotes vigorous debate about project risks but also has authority over budgets. The board establishes cost and time reserves to be set aside for each project component according to its degree of innovativeness. A simple extension from a prior mission would require a 10% to 20% financial reserve, for instance, whereas an entirely new component that had yet to work on Earth—much less on an unexplored planet—could require a 50% to 75% contingency. The reserves ensure that when problems inevitably arise, the project team has access to the money and time needed to resolve them without jeopardizing the launch date. JPL takes the estimates seriously; projects have been deferred or canceled if funds were insufficient to cover recommended reserves.

Facilitators
Many organizations, such as traditional energy and water utilities, operate in stable technological and market environments, with relatively predictable customer demand. In these situations risks stem largely from seemingly unrelated operational choices across a complex organization that accumulate gradually and can remain hidden for a long time.

Since no single staff group has the knowledge to perform operational-level risk management across diverse functions, firms may deploy a relatively small central risk-management group that collects information from operating managers. This increases managers' awareness of the risks that have been taken on across the organization and provides decision makers with a full picture of the company's risk profile.

We observed this model in action at Hydro One, the Canadian electricity company. Chief risk officer John Fraser, with the explicit backing of the CEO, runs dozens of workshops each year at which employees from all levels and functions identify and rank the principal risks they see to the company's strategic objectives. Employees use an anonymous voting technology to rate each risk, on a scale of 1 to 5, in terms of its impact, the likelihood of occurrence, and the strength of existing controls. The rankings are discussed in the workshops, and employees are empowered to voice and debate their risk perceptions. The group ultimately develops a consensus view that gets recorded on a visual risk map, recommends action plans, and designates an "owner" for each major risk.

Hydro One strengthens accountability by linking capital allocation and budgeting decisions to identified risks. The corporate-level capital-planning process allocates hundreds of millions of dollars, principally to projects that reduce risk effectively and efficiently. The risk group draws upon technical experts to challenge line engineers' investment plans and risk assessments and to provide independent expert oversight to the resource allocation process. At the annual capital allocation meeting, line managers have to defend their proposals in front of their peers and top executives. Managers want their projects to attract funding in the risk-based capital planning process, so they learn to overcome their bias to hide or minimize the risks in their areas of accountability.

Embedded experts

The financial services industry poses a unique challenge because of the volatile dynamics of asset markets and the potential impact of decisions made by decentralized traders and investment managers. An investment bank's risk profile can change dramatically with a single deal or major market movement. For such companies, risk management requires embedded experts within the organization to continuously monitor and influence the business's risk profile, working side by side with the line managers whose activities are generating new ideas, innovation, and risks—and, if all goes well, profits.

JP Morgan Private Bank adopted this model in 2007, at the onset of the global financial crisis. Risk managers, embedded within the line organization, report to both line executives and a centralized, independent risk-management function. The face-to-face contact with line managers enables the market-savvy risk managers to continually ask "what if" questions, challenging the assumptions of portfolio managers and forcing them to look at different scenarios. Risk managers assess how proposed trades affect the risk of the entire investment portfolio, not only under normal circumstances but also under times of extreme stress, when the correlations of returns across different asset classes escalate. "Portfolio managers come to me with three trades, and the [risk] model may say that all three are adding to the same type of risk," explains Gregoriy Zhikarev, a risk manager at JP Morgan. "Nine times out of 10 a manager will say, 'No, that's not what I want to do.' Then we can sit down and redesign the trades."

The chief danger from embedding risk managers within the line organization is that they "go native," aligning themselves with the inner circle of the business unit's leadership team—becoming deal makers rather than deal questioners. Preventing this is the responsibility of the company's senior risk officer and—ultimately—the CEO, who sets the tone for a company's risk culture.

Avoiding the Function Trap

Even if managers have a system that promotes rich discussions about risk, a second cognitive-behavioral trap awaits them. Because many strategy risks (and some external risks) are quite predictable—even familiar—companies tend to label and compartmentalize them, especially along business function lines. Banks often manage what they label "credit risk," "market risk," and "operational risk" in separate groups. Other companies compartmentalize the management of "brand risk," "reputation risk," "supply chain risk," "human resources risk," "IT risk," and "financial risk."

Such organizational silos disperse both information and responsibility for effective risk management. They inhibit discussion of how different risks interact. Good risk discussions must be not only confrontational but also integrative. Businesses can be derailed by a combination of small events that reinforce one another in unanticipated ways.

Managers can develop a companywide risk perspective by anchoring their discussions in strategic planning, the one integrative process that most well-run companies already have. For example, Infosys, the Indian IT services company, generates risk discussions from the Balanced Scorecard, its management tool for strategy measurement and communication. "As we asked ourselves about what risks we should be looking at," says M.D. Ranganath, the chief risk officer, "we gradually zeroed in on risks to business objectives specified in our corporate scorecard."

In building its Balanced Scorecard, Infosys had identified "growing client relationships" as a key objective and selected metrics for measuring progress, such as the number of global clients with annual billings in excess of $50 million and the annual percentage increases in revenues from large clients. In looking at the goal and the performance metrics together, management realized that its strategy had introduced a new risk factor: client default. When Infosys's business was based on numerous small clients, a single client default would not jeopardize the company's strategy. But a default by a $50 million client would present a major setback. Infosys began to monitor the credit default swap rate of every large client as a leading indicator of the likelihood of default. When a client's rate increased, Infosys would accelerate collection of receivables or request progress payments to reduce the likelihood or impact of default.

To take another example, consider Volkswagen do Brasil (subsequently abbreviated as VW), the Brazilian subsidiary of the

German carmaker. VW's risk-management unit uses the company's strategy map as a starting point for its dialogues about risk. For each objective on the map, the group identifies the risk events that could cause VW to fall short of that objective. The team then generates a Risk Event Card for each risk on the map, listing the practical effects of the event on operations, the probability of occurrence, leading indicators, and potential actions for mitigation. It also identifies who has primary accountability for managing the risk. (See the exhibit "The Risk Event Card.") The risk team then presents a high-level summary of results to senior management. (See "The Risk Report Card.")

Beyond introducing a systematic process for identifying and mitigating strategy risks, companies also need a risk oversight structure. Infosys uses a dual structure: a central risk team that identifies general strategy risks and establishes central policy, and specialized functional teams that design and monitor policies and controls in consultation with local business teams. The decentralized teams have the authority and expertise to help the business lines respond to threats and changes in their risk profiles, escalating only the exceptions to the central risk team for review. For example, if a client relationship manager wants to give a longer credit period to a company whose credit risk parameters are high, the functional risk manager can send the case to the central team for review.

These examples show that the size and scope of the risk function are not dictated by the size of the organization. Hydro One, a large company, has a relatively small risk group to generate risk awareness and communication throughout the firm and to advise the executive team on risk-based resource allocations. By contrast, relatively small companies or units, such as JPL or JP Morgan Private Bank, need multiple project-level review boards or teams of embedded risk managers to apply domain expertise to assess the risk of business decisions. And Infosys, a large company with broad operational and strategic scope, requires a strong centralized risk-management function as well as dispersed risk managers who support local business decisions and facilitate the exchange of information with the centralized risk group.

The Risk Event Card

VW do Brasil uses risk event cards to assess its strategy risks. First, managers document the risks associated with achieving each of the company's strategic objectives. For each identified risk, managers create a risk card that lists the practical effects of the event's occurring on operations. Below is a sample card looking at the effects of an interruption in deliveries, which could jeopardize VW's strategic objective of achieving a smoothly functioning supply chain.

Strategic objective	Risk event	Outcomes	Risk indicators	Likelihood/ Consequences	Management controls	Accountable manager
Guarantee reliable and competitive supplier-to-manufacturer processes	Interruption of deliveries	Overtime Emergency freight Quality problems Production losses	Critical items report Late deliveries Incoming defects Incorrect component shipments	(grid with X marked) 1 2 3 4 5	Hold daily supply chain meeting with logistics, purchasing, and QA Monitor suppliers' tooling to detect deterioration Risk mitigation initiative: Upgrade suppliers' tooling Risk mitigation initiative: Identify the key supply chain executive at each critical supplier	Mr. O. Manuel, director of manufacturing logistics

The Risk Report Card

VW do Brasil summarizes its strategy risks on a Risk Report Card organized by strategic objectives (excerpt below). Managers can see at a glance how many of the identified risks for each objective are critical and require attention or mitigation. For instance, VW identified 11 risks associated with achieving the goal "Satisfy the customer's expectations." Four of the risks were critical, but that was an improvement over the previous quarter's assessment. Managers can also monitor progress on risk management across the company.

Strategic objective	Assessed risks	Critical risks	Trend
Achieve market share growth	4	1	↔
Satisfy the customer's expectations	11	4	↑
Improve company image	13	1	↔
Develop dealer organization	4	2	↔
Guarantee customer-oriented innovations management	5	2	↓
Achieve launch management efficiency	1	0	↔
Increase direct processes efficiency	4	1	↔
Create and manage a robust production volume strategy	2	1	↓
Guarantee reliable and competitive supplier-to-manufacturer processes	9	3	↔
Develop an attractive and innovative product portfolio	4	2	↓

Managing the Uncontrollable

External risks, the third category of risk, cannot typically be reduced or avoided through the approaches used for managing preventable and strategy risks. External risks lie largely outside the company's control; companies should focus on identifying them, assessing their potential impact, and figuring out how best to mitigate their effects should they occur.

Some external risk events are sufficiently imminent that managers can manage them as they do their strategy risks. For example, during the economic slowdown after the global financial crisis, Infosys identified a new risk related to its objective of developing a global workforce: an upsurge in protectionism, which could lead to tight restrictions on work visas and permits for foreign nationals in several OECD countries where Infosys had large client engagements. Although protectionist legislation is technically an external risk since it's beyond the company's control, Infosys treated it as a strategy risk and created a Risk Event Card for it, which included a new risk indicator: the number and percentage of its employees with dual citizenships or existing work permits outside India. If this number were to fall owing to staff turnover, Infosys's global strategy might be jeopardized. Infosys therefore put in place recruiting and retention policies that mitigate the consequences of this external risk event.

Most external risk events, however, require a different analytic approach either because their probability of occurrence is very low or because managers find it difficult to envision them during their normal strategy processes. We have identified several different sources of external risks:

- *Natural and economic disasters with immediate impact.* These risks are predictable in a general way, although their timing is usually not (a large earthquake will hit someday in California, but there is no telling exactly where or when). They may be anticipated only by relatively weak signals. Examples include natural disasters such as the 2010 Icelandic volcano eruption that closed European airspace for a week and economic disasters such as the bursting of a major asset price bubble. When these risks occur, their effects are typically drastic and immediate, as we saw in the disruption from the Japanese earthquake and tsunami in 2011.

- *Geopolitical and environmental changes with long-term impact.* These include political shifts such as major policy changes, coups, revolutions, and wars; long-term environmental changes such as global warming; and depletion of critical natural resources such as fresh water.

- *Competitive risks with medium-term impact.* These include the emergence of disruptive technologies (such as the internet, smartphones, and bar codes) and radical strategic moves by industry players (such as the entry of Amazon into book retailing and Apple into the mobile phone and consumer electronics industries).

Companies use different analytic approaches for each of the sources of external risk.

Tail-risk stress tests

Stress-testing helps companies assess major changes in one or two specific variables whose effects would be major and immediate, although the exact timing is not forecastable. Financial services firms use stress tests to assess, for example, how an event such as the tripling of oil prices, a large swing in exchange or interest rates, or the default of a major institution or sovereign country would affect trading positions and investments.

The benefits from stress-testing, however, depend critically on the assumptions—which may themselves be biased—about how much the variable in question will change. The tail-risk stress tests of many banks in 2007–2008, for example, assumed a worst-case scenario in which U.S. housing prices leveled off and remained flat for several periods. Very few companies thought to test what would happen if prices began to decline—an excellent example of the tendency to anchor estimates in recent and readily available data. Most companies extrapolated from recent U.S. housing prices, which had gone several decades without a general decline, to develop overly optimistic market assessments.

Scenario planning

This tool is suited for long-range analysis, typically five to 10 years out. Originally developed at Shell Oil in the 1960s, scenario analysis is a systematic process for defining the plausible boundaries of future states of the world. Participants examine political, economic, technological, social, regulatory, and environmental forces and select some number of drivers—typically four—that would have the biggest impact on the company. Some companies explicitly draw on the expertise in their advisory boards to inform them about significant trends, outside the company's and industry's day-to-day focus, that should be considered in their scenarios.

For each of the selected drivers, participants estimate maximum and minimum anticipated values over five to 10 years. Combining the extreme values for each of four drivers leads to 16 scenarios. About half tend to be implausible and are discarded; participants then assess how their firm's strategy would perform in the remaining scenarios. If managers see that their strategy is contingent on a generally optimistic view, they can modify it to accommodate pessimistic scenarios or develop plans for how they would change their strategy should early indicators show an increasing likelihood of events turning against it.

War-gaming

War-gaming assesses a firm's vulnerability to disruptive technologies or changes in competitors' strategies. In a war-game, the company assigns three or four teams the task of devising plausible near-term strategies or actions that existing or potential competitors might adopt during the next one or two years—a shorter time horizon than that of scenario analysis. The teams then meet to examine how clever competitors could attack the company's strategy. The process helps to overcome the bias of leaders to ignore evidence that runs counter to their current beliefs, including the possibility of actions that competitors might take to disrupt their strategy.

Companies have no influence over the likelihood of risk events identified through methods such as tail-risk testing, scenario planning, and war-gaming. But managers can take specific actions to mitigate their impact. Since moral hazard does not arise for non-preventable events, companies can use insurance or hedging to mitigate some risks, as an airline does when it protects itself against sharp increases in fuel prices by using financial derivatives. Another option is for firms to make investments now to avoid much higher costs later. For instance, a manufacturer with facilities in earthquake-prone areas can increase its construction costs to protect critical facilities against severe quakes. Also, companies exposed to different but comparable risks can cooperate to mitigate them. For example, the IT data centers of a university in North Carolina would be vulnerable to hurricane risk while those of a comparable university on the San Andreas Fault in California would be vulnerable to earthquakes. The likelihood that both disasters would happen on the same day is small enough that the two universities might choose to mitigate their risks by backing up each other's systems every night.

The Leadership Challenge

Managing risk is very different from managing strategy. Risk management focuses on the negative—threats and failures rather than opportunities and successes. It runs exactly counter to the "can do" culture most leadership teams try to foster when implementing strategy. And many leaders have a tendency to discount the future; they're reluctant to spend time and money now to avoid an uncertain future problem that might occur down the road, on someone else's watch. Moreover, mitigating risk typically involves dispersing resources and diversifying investments, just the opposite of the intense focus of a successful strategy. Managers may find it antithetical to their culture to champion processes that identify the risks to the strategies they helped to formulate.

For those reasons, most companies need a separate function to handle strategy- and external-risk management. The risk function's size will vary from company to company, but the group must report directly to the top team. Indeed, nurturing a close relationship with senior leadership will arguably be its most critical task; a company's ability to weather storms depends very much on how seriously executives take their risk-management function when the sun is shining and no clouds are on the horizon.

That was what separated the banks that failed in the financial crisis from those that survived. The failed companies had relegated risk management to a compliance function; their risk managers had limited access to senior management and their boards of directors. Further, executives routinely ignored risk managers' warnings about highly leveraged and concentrated positions. By contrast, Goldman Sachs and JPMorgan Chase, two firms that weathered the financial crisis well, had strong internal risk-management functions and leadership teams that understood and managed the companies' multiple risk exposures. Barry Zubrow, chief risk officer at JP Morgan Chase, told us, "I may have the title, but [CEO] Jamie Dimon is the chief risk officer of the company."

Risk management is nonintuitive; it runs counter to many individual and organizational biases. Rules and compliance can mitigate some critical risks but not all of them. Active and cost-effective risk management requires managers to think systematically about the multiple categories of risks they face so that they can institute appropriate processes for each. These processes will neutralize their managerial bias of seeing the world as they would like it to be rather than as it actually is or could possibly become.

Originally published in June 2012. Reprint R1206B

21st-Century Talent Spotting

by Claudio Fernández-Aráoz

A FEW YEARS AGO, I was asked to help find a new CEO for a family-owned electronics retailer that wanted to professionalize its management and expand its operations. I worked closely with the outgoing chief executive and the board to pinpoint the relevant competencies for the job and then seek out and assess candidates. The man we hired had all the right credentials: He'd attended top professional schools and worked for some of the best organizations in the industry, and he was a successful country manager in one of the world's most admired companies. Even more important, he'd scored above the target level for each of the competencies we'd identified. But none of that mattered. Despite his impressive background and great fit, he could not adjust to the massive technological, competitive, and regulatory changes occurring in the market at the time. Following three years of lackluster performance, he was asked to leave.

Compare that story with one from the start of my executive search career. My task was to fill a project manager role at a small brewery owned by Quinsa, which then dominated the beer market in the southern cone of Latin America. In those days, I hadn't yet heard the term "competency." I was working in a new office without research support (in the pre-internet era), and Quinsa was the only serious beverage industry player in the region, so I was simply unable to identify a large pool of people with the right industry and functional background. Ultimately, I contacted Pedro Algorta, an executive I'd met in 1981, while we were both studying at Stanford University. A survivor of the infamous 1972 plane crash in the Andes, which has been chronicled in several books and the movie *Alive,* Algorta was certainly an interesting choice. But he had no experience in the consumer goods business; was unfamiliar with Corrientes, the province where the brewery was located; and had never worked in marketing or sales, key areas of expertise. Still, I had a feeling he would be successful, and Quinsa agreed to hire him. That decision proved to be a smart one. Algorta was rapidly promoted to general manager of the Corrientes brewery and then CEO of Quinsa's flagship Quilmes brewery. He also became a key member of the team that transformed Quinsa from a family-owned enterprise to a large, respected conglomerate with a management team considered at the time to be among the best in Latin America.

Why did the CEO of the electronics business, who seemed so right for the position, fail so miserably? And why did Algorta, so clearly unqualified, succeed so spectacularly? The answer is *potential:* the ability to adapt to and grow into increasingly complex roles and environments. Algorta had it; the first CEO did not.

Having spent 30 years evaluating and tracking executives and studying the factors in their performance, I now consider potential to be the most important predictor of success at all levels, from junior management to the C-suite and the board. I've learned how to identify people who have it and to help companies develop and deploy them. With this article, I share those lessons. As business becomes more volatile and complex, and the global market for top professionals gets tighter, I am convinced that organizations and their leaders must transition to what I think of as a new era of talent spotting—one in which our evaluations of one another are based not on brawn, brains, experience, or competencies, but on potential.

A New Era

The first era of talent spotting lasted millennia. For thousands of years, humans made choices about one another on the basis of

Idea in Brief

The Problem

In the past few decades, organizations have emphasized "competencies" in hiring and developing talent. Jobs have been decomposed into skills and filled by candidates who have them. But 21st-century business is too volatile and complex—and the market for top talent too tight—for that model to work anymore.

The Solution

Today those responsible for hiring and promotion decisions

must instead focus on potential: the ability to adapt to ever-changing business environments and grow into challenging new roles.

The Tools

Managers must learn to assess current and prospective employees on five key indicators: the right motivation, curiosity, insight, engagement, and determination. Then they have to help the best get better with smart retention and stretch assignments.

physical attributes. If you wanted to erect a pyramid, dig a canal, fight a war, or harvest a crop, you chose the fittest, healthiest, strongest people you could find. Those attributes were easy to assess, and, despite their growing irrelevance, we still unconsciously look for them: *Fortune* 500 CEOs are on average 2.5 inches taller than the average American, and the statistics on military leaders and country presidents are similar.

I was born and raised during the second era, which emphasized intelligence, experience, and past performance. Throughout much of the 20th century, IQ—verbal, analytical, mathematical, and logical cleverness—was justifiably seen as an important factor in hiring processes (particularly for white-collar roles), with educational pedigrees and tests used as proxies. Much work also became standardized and professionalized. Many kinds of workers could be certified with reliability and transparency, and since most roles were relatively similar across companies and industries, and from year to year, past performance was considered a fine indicator. If you were looking for an engineer, accountant, lawyer, designer, or CEO, you would scout out, interview, and hire the smartest, most experienced engineer, accountant, lawyer, designer, or CEO.

I joined the executive search profession in the 1980s, at the beginning of the third era of talent spotting, which was driven by the competency movement still prevalent today. David McClelland's 1973 paper "Testing for Competence Rather than for 'Intelligence'" proposed that workers, especially managers, be evaluated on specific characteristics and skills that helped predict outstanding performance in the roles for which they were being hired. The time was right for such thinking, because technological evolution and industry convergence had made jobs much more complex, often rendering experience and performance in previous positions irrelevant. So, instead, we decomposed jobs into competencies and looked for candidates with the right combination of them. For leadership roles, we also began to rely on research showing that emotional intelligence was even more important than IQ.

Now we're at the dawn of a fourth era, in which the focus must shift to potential. In a volatile, uncertain, complex, and ambiguous environment (VUCA is the military-acronym-turned-corporate-buzzword), competency-based appraisals and appointments are increasingly insufficient. What makes someone successful in a particular role today might not tomorrow if the competitive environment shifts, the company's strategy changes, or he or she must collaborate with or manage a different group of colleagues. So the question is not whether your company's employees and leaders have the right skills; it's whether they have the potential to learn new ones.

The Scarcity of Top Talent

Unfortunately, potential is much harder to discern than competence (though not impossible, as I'll describe later). Moreover, your organization will be looking for it in what will soon be one of the toughest employment markets in history—for employers, not job seekers. The recent noise about high unemployment rates in the United States and Europe hides important signals: Three forces—globalization, demographics, and pipelines—will make senior talent ever scarcer in the years to come.

Back in 2006, I worked with Nitin Nohria, the current dean of Harvard Business School, and my Egon Zehnder colleagues to study this issue, gathering detailed data and interviewing CEOs from 47 companies with a combined market capitalization of $2 trillion, revenue of over $1 trillion, and more than 3 million employees. Representing all major sectors and geographies, these firms were successful, with strong reputations and solid people practices. Yet we found that all were about to face a massive talent crunch. Eight years later, the situation for companies is just as bad, if not worse.

Let's examine the three factors in turn. *Globalization* compels companies to reach beyond their home markets and to compete for the people who can help them do so. The major global firms in our 2006 study anticipated an 88% increase in their proportion of revenue from developing regions by 2012. Not only did that happen, but the International Monetary Fund and other groups are currently predicting that some 70% of the world's growth between now and 2016 will come from emerging markets. At the same time, firms in developing nations are themselves vying for talent, as well as customers, around the world. Take China, which now has 88 companies in the global *Fortune* 500, up from just eight in 2003, thanks in part to foreign growth. Huawei, the leading Chinese telecommunications company, employs more than 70,000 people, 45% of whom work in R&D centers in countries including Germany, Sweden, the U.S., France, Italy, Russia, and India. Similar examples can be found in companies based in markets such as India and Brazil.

The impact of *demographics* on hiring pools is also undeniable. The sweet spot for rising senior executives is the 35-to-44-year-old age bracket, but the percentage of people in that range is shrinking dramatically. In our 2006 study, we calculated that a projected 30% decline in the ranks of young leaders, combined with anticipated business growth, would cut in half the pool of senior leader candidates in that critical age group. Whereas a decade ago this demographic shift was affecting mostly the United States and Europe, by 2020 many other countries, including Russia, Canada, South Korea, and China, will have more people at retirement age than entering the workforce.

Potential at the Top

A FOCUS ON POTENTIAL can improve talent spotting at every level of the organization—especially the very top. When choosing a CEO or board member, as opposed to a young manager, you'll often find that several candidates have the right credentials, experience, and competencies. That's why an accurate assessment of their motivation, curiosity, insight, engagement, and determination is all the more important.

For CEO roles, succession planning must start very early, ideally when a new leader takes charge but no later than three to four years before he or she expects to leave. At Egon Zehnder, even when a much longer tenure is expected, we help companies assess potential two to four layers below the C-suite, identifying people to retain and develop so that some can become contenders for the top job.

I know one outstanding corporate director who twice orchestrated the dismissal of fully competent C-suite executives because they didn't have enough potential and she wanted to make their roles—key development opportunities—available to people who did. Board appointments require the same discipline. Our firm's UK office recently helped a highly respected retail group, the John Lewis Partnership, evaluate a long list of candidates for two nonexecutive director positions, using all the indicators of potential—curiosity, in particular—as key metrics. After all, if a company's leaders don't have the potential to learn, grow, and adapt to new environments, how can they attract up-and-coming employees and managers who do?

The third phenomenon is related and equally powerful, but much less well known: Companies are not properly developing their *pipelines* of future leaders. In PricewaterhouseCoopers's 2014 survey of CEOs in 68 countries, 63% of respondents said they were concerned about the future availability of key skills at all levels. The Boston Consulting Group cites proprietary research showing that 56% of executives see critical gaps in their ability to fill senior managerial roles in coming years. HBS professor Boris Groysberg found similar concerns in his 2013 survey of executive program participants: Respondents gave their companies' leadership pipelines an average rating of 3.2 out of 5, compared with an average score of 4 for current CEOs and 3.8 for current top teams. Equally troubling were responses to other kinds of questions in the survey: No talent management function was rated higher than 3.3, and critical employee development activities, such as job rotations, were scored as low as 2.6. In other words, few executives think their companies are doing a good job identifying and developing qualified leaders. Recent executive panel interviews conducted by my colleagues confirm that this view is widespread. Only 22% of the 823 leaders who participated consider their pipelines promising, and only 19% said they find it easy to attract the best talent.

In many companies, particularly those based in developed markets, I've found that half of senior leaders will be eligible for retirement within the next two years, and half of them don't have a successor ready or able to take over. As Groysberg puts it, "Companies may not be feeling pain today, but in five or 10 years, as people retire or move on, where will the next generation of leaders come from?"

Taken independently, globalization, demographics, and pipelines would each create unprecedented demand for talent over the next decade. The pace of globalization has never been faster; the imbalance between old and young has never been so dramatic; views on the pipelines of qualified successors have never been more negative; and the survey ratings of development practices are the lowest I've seen. Combine all those factors, and you get a war for talent that will present a huge, perhaps insurmountable, challenge for most organizations. But for those that learn how to spot potential, effectively retain people who have it, and create development programs to help the best get better, the situation will instead offer an extraordinary opportunity.

Better Hiring

The first step is to get the right people into your organization. As Amazon CEO Jeff Bezos, one of the most impressive corporate value creators in recent history, put it in 1998, "Setting the bar high in our approach to hiring has been, and will continue to be, the single most important element of [our] success." So, when evaluating job candidates (and reevaluating current employees), how do you gauge potential?

Many companies have well-established "high potential" programs, through which they fast-track promising managers for development and promotions. But most of these are actually "high performer" programs, full of people who have done well in the past and are therefore assumed to have the best shot of doing well in the future—but given VUCA conditions, that is no longer a safe prediction. About 80% of the participants in the executive programs I teach consistently report that their companies don't use an empirically validated model for assessing potential. I'll admit, this kind of evaluation is much more difficult than measuring IQ, past performance, and even various competencies. But it can be done—with a predictive accuracy around 85%, according to data on the careers of thousands of executives we assessed at Egon Zehnder using a model developed and refined over the past two decades.

The first indicator of potential we look for is the right kind of *motivation:* a fierce commitment to excel in the pursuit of unselfish goals. High potentials have great ambition and want to leave their mark, but they also aspire to big, collective goals, show deep personal humility, and invest in getting better at everything they do. We consider motivation first because it is a stable—and usually unconscious—quality. If someone is driven purely by selfish motives, that probably won't change.

We then consider four other qualities that are hallmarks of potential, according to our research:

- *Curiosity:* a penchant for seeking out new experiences, knowledge, and candid feedback and an openness to learning and change

- *Insight:* the ability to gather and make sense of information that suggests new possibilities

- *Engagement:* a knack for using emotion and logic to communicate a persuasive vision and connect with people

- *Determination:* the wherewithal to fight for difficult goals despite challenges and to bounce back from adversity

In retrospect, I can see that Pedro Algorta succeeded at Quinsa because he had all those qualities, not because he possessed a specific set of skills and competencies. And those qualities were in high relief during his harrowing ordeal in the Andes. He demonstrated his motivation by playing a critical yet humble role—providing sustenance for the explorers who would eventually march out to save the group. He melted snow for them to drink and cut and dried small pieces of flesh from the dead bodies of fellow victims to serve as food. Instead of succumbing to despair, Algorta became curious about the environment around him, taking an interest in the water coming off the ice. It flowed east, leading him, and only him, to the insight that the dying pilot had misreported their position; they were on the Argentine side of the mountain range, not on the Chilean side. His engagement and determination were also clear over those 72 days. He faithfully tended to his dying friend, Arturo Nogueira, who had suffered multiple leg fractures, trying to distract the young man from his pain. He encouraged his fellow survivors to maintain hope and persuaded them all to condone the consumption of their own bodies, should they die, describing it as "an act of love."

Although Algorta's tenure as CEO bears no resemblance to what he experienced on that mountain, the same characteristics served him in his career at Quinsa. Perhaps the best example of the purity of his motives came at the end of his 10-year stint with the company, when, for sound strategic reasons, he recommended that it abandon the agribusiness project he was leading, thus voting himself out of a job. He was also a curious executive, always going out of his way to meet customers, clients, and workers at all levels, and to listen to voices that usually went unheard. As a result, he accepted and supported some revolutionary marketing initiatives, which allowed Quilmes to multiply its sales eightfold while achieving record profitability. He displayed great insight both in his hiring decisions—the future CEOs of both Quilmes and Nestlé were among his best hires—and in his strategic ones: for example, his bold move to divest all noncore assets so that the company could use the proceeds to expand the regional brewery business. His engagement transformed an ineffective and even vicious culture at Quilmes; his insistence that bosses and subordinates come together in open meetings set a precedent that was later rolled out to the whole group. Finally, Algorta showed amazing determination at Quinsa. When the project he'd been hired to lead—the construction of a new brewery—ran out of funds just after he took over, he didn't consider quitting; instead, he pushed to get the necessary financing. And when Argentina was shaken by devaluation and hyperinflation a few months later, he pressed on; the facility was up and running in 15 months.

How can you tell if a candidate you've just met—or a current employee—has potential? By mining his or her personal and professional history, as I've just done with Algorta's. Conduct in-depth interviews or career discussions, and do thorough reference checks to uncover stories that demonstrate whether the person has (or lacks) these qualities. For instance, to assess curiosity, don't just ask, "Are you curious?" Instead, look for signs that the person believes in self-improvement, truly enjoys learning, and is able to recalibrate after missteps. Questions like the following can help:

- How do you react when someone challenges you?

- How do you invite input from others on your team?

- What do you do to broaden your thinking, experience, or personal development?

- How do you foster learning in your organization?

- What steps do you take to seek out the unknown?

Always ask for concrete examples, and go just as deep in your exploration of motivation, insight, engagement, and determination. Your conversations with managers, colleagues, and direct reports who know the person well should be just as detailed.

As a leader, you must also work to spread these interviewing techniques through the organization. Researchers have found that while the best interviewers' assessments have a very high positive correlation with the candidates' ultimate performance, some interviewers' opinions are worse than flipping a coin. Still, few managers learn proper assessment techniques from their business schools or their employers; in my surveys of participants in executive talent management programs, I've found that only about 30% think that their companies provide adequate training. Most organizations, it seems, are filled with people who have the power to endorse bad candidates and kill off good ones.

By contrast, companies that emphasize the right kind of hiring vastly improve their odds. Amazon has, for example, hundreds of dedicated internal recruiters, great training programs in assessment, and even a legion of certified "bar raisers": skilled evaluators who hold full-time jobs in a range of departments but are also empowered to participate in assessing—and vetoing—candidates for other areas.

The Brazilian mining group Companhia Vale do Rio Doce, known as Vale, took a similarly disciplined approach, working with Egon Zehnder, during the 2001 to 2011 tenure of CEO Roger Agnelli. On his watch, not one senior role was filled without an objective, independent, and professional assessment of all internal and external candidates. Managers were encouraged to favor motivated, curious, insightful, engaging, and determined prospects even when they had no specific experience in the field or function to which they had applied. "We would never choose someone who was not passionate and committed to our long-term strategy and demanding objectives," Agnelli explains. Some 250 executives were hired or promoted in this way, all over the world, and the strategy paid off. Vale became a global player in the mining industry, dramatically outperforming others in the country and the region.

Smart Retention

Once you've hired true high potentials and identified the ones you already have, you'll need to focus on keeping them. After all, competitors grappling with the same tight talent market will be more than happy to tempt them away. Agnelli says his proudest achievement at Vale was not the huge revenue, profit, and share price growth over which he presided but the improved quality of the leaders rising through the company's ranks. "After five or six years, everyone appointed at the highest levels came from inside," he says, adding that the capacity to build and retain great teams is *"the* key" to any leader's or organization's success.

Indeed, when the Brazilian government used its 61% stake in Vale's controlling shares to precipitate Agnelli's departure, in 2011, prompting the voluntary resignations of seven out of eight executive committee members within a year, the company soon lost almost half its value. Growing disenchantment with Brazilian and commodity stocks played a role, to be sure. But given that Vale's closest competitors, Rio Tinto and BHP Billiton, saw much less dramatic declines over the same period, it seems clear that investors were also reacting to the loss of an outstanding leadership team.

How can you emulate Vale under Agnelli and avoid the company's subsequent fate? By considering what your high potentials want most from you. As Daniel H. Pink explains in *Drive,* most of us (especially knowledge workers) are energized by three fundamental things: *autonomy*—the freedom to direct our lives; *mastery*—our craving to excel; and *purpose*—the yearning for our work to serve something larger than ourselves.

Pay does matter, of course. All employees, especially rising stars, expect their compensation to reflect their contribution or effort and to be comparable to that of others doing similar jobs. However, in my experience, while unfair pay can surely demotivate, compensation beyond a certain level is much less important than most people think. In my examination of candidates hired through our firm who were successful in their new jobs but moved on within three years, I found that 85% of them were hired away into a more senior position, confirming that they were competent people with potential. But only 4% of them cited more money as the primary reason for their departures. More common reasons were bad bosses, limited support, and lack of opportunities for growth.

So do pay your stars fairly, ideally above the average. But also give them autonomy in four "T" dimensions: task (what they do), time (when they do it), team (whom they do it with), and technique (how they do it). Help them toward mastery by setting difficult but attainable challenges and eliminating distractions. And engage them in a greater team, organizational, or societal goal. Bezos and other leaders at Amazon are expert at this. Agnelli and his team at Vale were, too. But the conditions at the company following his departure failed to motivate the remaining leaders in the same way, and many of them chose to move on.

Stretch Development

Your final job is to make sure your stars live up to the high potential you've spotted in them by offering development opportunities that push them out of their comfort zones. Jonathan Harvey, a top HR executive at ANZ, an Australian bank that operates in 33 countries, puts it this way: "When it comes to developing executives for future leadership assignments, we're constantly striving to find the optimal level of discomfort in the next role or project, because that's where the most learning happens. We don't want people to be stretched beyond their limits. But we want well-rounded, values-focused leaders who see the world through a wide-angle lens, and the right stretch assignments are what helps people get there."

To explain the consequences of *not* challenging your high potentials, I often point to Japan. In 2008 Kentaro Aramaki, from Egon Zehnder's Tokyo office, and I mapped the potential of senior Japanese executives (that is, our consultants' objective assessments of the executives' ability to take on bigger roles and responsibilities, as measured by the indicators described above) against their competence (that is, our objective assessments of the eight leadership competencies listed in the sidebar "What Else Should You Look For?"). When we compared those scores with the average scores of all executives in our worldwide database, we found a great paradox. Japanese professionals had higher potential than the global average but lower competence. In spite of great raw material, there was a poor final product. The problem was, and still is, Japan's flawed development process. Although the country's educational institutions and the strong work ethic that is part of Japanese culture give managers a jump-start in their careers, their growth is stymied when they actually start working. A leader in Japan traditionally rises through

What Else Should You Look For?

ALTHOUGH POTENTIAL SHOULD BE the defining measure of executives today, it would be a mistake to ignore other lessons we've learned over the years about how to evaluate people.

Intelligence

Although you probably won't administer an IQ test, it is important to assess a candidate's general intelligence (including analytical, verbal, mathematical, and logical reasoning) by considering educational background, early job experiences, and responses to interview questions. You don't need to look for geniuses; for most jobs anything above a certain level of intelligence has almost no impact on performance. However, you should still hire people clever enough for your requirements, because their general intelligence won't increase dramatically over time.

Values

Values are critical, and you can't expect to impart them on the job. Use interviews and reference checks not only to weigh the essentials, such as honesty and integrity, but also to discover if the candidate shares your organization's core values.

Leadership Abilities

Some competencies are relevant (though not sufficient) when evaluating senior manager candidates. While each job and organization is different, the best leaders have, in some measure, eight abilities.

---

the ranks of one division, in one company, waiting respectfully for promotions that usually come only when he's the most senior person in line for the spot.

Recently a Tokyo-based global conglomerate asked our firm to assess its top dozen senior leaders, all in their mid- to late 50s. This company, which operates in multiple industries and markets, should have been an ideal training ground for executives. However, only one of the managers we evaluated had worked in more than a single business line. The time each had spent working outside Japan was just one year, on average. And their English language skills were quite limited. As a result, none were suitable candidates to succeed the CEO. The

1. **Strategic orientation.** The capacity to engage in broad, complex analytical and conceptual thinking

2. **Market insight.** A strong understanding of the market and how it affects the business

3. **Results orientation.** A commitment to demonstrably improving key business metrics

4. **Customer impact.** A passion for serving the customer

5. **Collaboration and influence.** An ability to work effectively with peers or partners, including those not in the line of command

6. **Organizational development.** A drive to improve the company by attracting and developing top talent

7. **Team leadership.** Success in focusing, aligning, and building effective groups

8. **Change leadership.** The capacity to transform and align an organization around a new goal

You should assess these abilities through interviews and reference checks, in the same way you would evaluate potential, aiming to confirm that the candidate has displayed them in the past, under similar circumstances.

sad thing is that all had started off strong. They were engineers, with an average tenure of more than 20 years in R&D and product strategy and marketing—but that potential had been squandered.

Pushing your high potentials up a straight ladder toward bigger jobs, budgets, and staffs will continue their growth, but it won't accelerate it. Diverse, complex, challenging, uncomfortable roles will. When we recently asked 823 international executives to look back at their careers and tell us what had helped them unleash their potential, the most popular answer, cited by 71%, was stretch assignments. Job rotations and personal mentors, each mentioned by 49% of respondents, tied for second.

How do you make sure people in your organization are getting the stretch assignments and job rotations they need? Let's come back to ANZ. Following a 2007 to 2010 hiring spree as the company expanded across Asia, it decided to refine its leadership development processes. Its efforts center on what it calls business-critical roles: those that make a vital contribution to the strategic agenda; require a scarce set of skills; produce highly variable outcomes dependent on the incumbent; and, if vacant, pose a significant threat to business continuity and performance momentum.

ANZ makes a point of assessing all its managers for potential and then placing those who rate the highest in these business-critical roles. Other development initiatives include the Generalist Bankers Program, which each year offers 10 to 15 participants the opportunity to spend two years rotating through wholesale, commercial, and retail banking, risk, and operations to build broad industry and corporate knowledge. Participants then move into permanent roles with a focus on gaining geographic, cultural, product, and client-facing experience, including a mandatory posting in internal audit to ensure that they understand the bank's control frameworks. The program commitment is 15 years, with the goal of a country CEO posting at the end.

This disciplined approach already seems to be bearing fruit. Whereas three years ago 70% of ANZ's senior executive roles were filled by external candidates, outside hiring is now below 20%. Internal surveys show that staff engagement has increased from 64% to 72%, while "same-period performance excellence" (a measure of employee commitment to customer service and product quality) has jumped from 68% to 78%. And the business has benefited in other ways. In 2013 the company was judged the number four international bank in the Asia Pacific region for the second consecutive year by the highly regarded Greenwich customer survey, up from number 12 in 2008.

———————

Geopolitics, business, industries, and jobs are changing so rapidly that we can't predict the competencies needed to succeed even a few years out. It is therefore imperative to identify and develop people with the highest potential. Look for those who have a strong motivation to excel in the pursuit of challenging goals, along with the humility to put the group ahead of individual needs; an insatiable curiosity that propels them to explore new ideas and avenues; keen insight that allows them to see connections where others don't; a strong engagement with their work and the people around them; and the determination to overcome setbacks and obstacles. That doesn't mean forgetting about factors like intelligence, experience, performance, and specific competencies, particularly the ones related to leadership. But hiring for potential and effectively retaining and developing those who have it—at every level of the organization—should now be your top priority.

Originally published in June 2014. Reprint R1406B

How CEOs Can Work with an Active Board

by Ken Banta and Stephen D. Garrow

AT COMPANIES OF ALMOST ALL SIZES, across all sectors, boards are undergoing a profound transformation. Largely as a result of intensifying shareholder intolerance of mediocre or poor corporate performance, the ceremonial boards of the past are being replaced by active boards that are more demanding of executives and more intrusive in their affairs.

This change can be daunting and frustrating for CEOs. However, based on our experience of advising CEOs, operating as CEOs, and sitting on boards, we have found that executives can be effective in the new environment by revamping their interactions with their boards. Doing so consists of four approaches.

Work with board members individually as well as in the group—and selectively seek their help

It's remarkable how many CEOs focus mainly on formal boardroom relationships. Yet by investing the time in regular one-to-one informal interactions, a CEO will help address the new active board members' sense of duty to get close to the business. Through a personal dialogue, the CEO can better enlist them in important initiatives and address issues before they become crises. In addition, by creating a personal bond with individual directors, the CEO lessens the odds that they will undermine or blindside him or her.

It is especially important to create a bond with both the lead director and the board chair. As boards have become more active, the lead director and board chair hold the keys to setting productive agendas and managing issues with the full board or individual members. One of us served on an active board that included members who frequently threatened to derail agendas and process with counterproductive questions. The CEO quietly recruited the lead director and chair to restore order, which they did.

CEOs should consider recruiting one board member as an informal adviser. This must be done with great care and an ear for political nuances. For example, as one CEO we know discovered, a prospective board adviser actually had his eye on the CEO role for himself—hardly the right confidant! By using already-scheduled one-on-ones to assess board members for this advisory role, the CEO can better identify an appropriate confidant. This board member can be of great value as a sounding board and a guide to working effectively with the rest of the board.

Communicate less formally, more intensively, more often

Many CEOs and their teams still deliver traditional 80-slide PowerPoint summary presentations at board meetings. But given that today's boards increasingly want a substantive dialogue, we advise replacing the presentation with a thoughtful verbal review and Q&A around critical updates, challenges, and opportunities. (Further background can be provided in brief prereading material.)

This will show that the CEO is using his or her face-to-face time with the board for serious discussion. It will focus board activism on topics where the CEO will benefit from directors' insight and counsel. And by taking the lead in inviting the board to engage on business-critical matters, the CEO can better manage the process and avoid one of the biggest downsides of the active board: disruptive interference by board members in business operations.

It may seem obvious that CEOs should communicate with board members regularly and substantively between board meetings. But

Idea in Brief

At companies of almost all sizes, across all sectors, boards are undergoing a profound transformation. Largely as a result of intensifying shareholder intolerance of mediocre or poor corporate performance, the ceremonial boards of the past are being replaced by active boards that are more demanding of managers and more intrusive in their affairs. This change can be daunting and frustrating for CEOs. However, based on our experience of advising CEOs, operating as CEOs, and sitting on boards, we have found that executives can be effective in the new environment by revamping their interactions with their boards. It consists of four approaches.

- Work with board members individually as well as in the group—and selectively seek their help

- Communicate less formally, more intensively, more often

- Expose Level 3 and 4 managers to the board.

- Handle strategic planning . . . strategically

in reality, CEOs often communicate mainly when there is a problem. Many also have difficulty regularly addressing a balanced mix of important topics.

One very effective approach to this issue is regular CEO letters to the board. The management of this letter should be delegated to a top lieutenant, such as the head of communications or the COO. A monthly rhythm has proven effective with many boards. To assure balanced, relevant content, the letter should routinely address a fixed set of regular topics (such as business-environment trends, business updates, people/talent news, and early warnings of potential upside and downside developments).

Expose level 3 and 4 managers to the board

While boards in the past were typically focused on CEO succession planning and the talent among the CEO's direct reports, active boards are also very interested in the levels below the C-suite. They rightly see these executives as the leaders of the future and the operational leaders of today who should be driving performance. Active board members will therefore seek to get to know them.

Some CEOs feel this is overly intrusive or worry that the lower-level executives are not ready for board exposure. But, in fact, it's beneficial to have board members engaging with deeper levels of talent. They learn more about the business and the next generation of the company's leaders. Board members can also give the CEO valuable feedback about the people they meet and their view of the company's overall bench strength. And for the executives, the right kind of exposure to board members is a great development opportunity.

The CEO should take the lead with the board in driving the engagement process, which will allow him or her to have greater influence over it. The CEO can select the highest-potential individuals for the interactions and organize the interactions so that they are most productive—for example, by holding them as one-to-ones over a breakfast or dinner. The CEO can also brief the executives in advance on the style of the board member and potential question areas and brief the board members on the executives they will meet.

Handle strategic planning . . . strategically

Older-style boards typically become involved only at the end of the strategic-planning process—typically in a board meeting devoted to review and approval of the strategy. By contrast, active boards often push to be involved from the start because the strategy is so important to the company's performance.

The notion of involving the board in strategic planning can make CEOs anxious and defensive. They fear that the board may undermine the planning process due to insufficient knowledge about the business. They also worry that board involvement in strategic planning will be the thin end of the wedge and lead to board interference in day-to-day management of the company.

The key to navigating this challenge is to keep strategic planning in the hands of management but to invite the board to provide advice and feedback from the beginning. One good way to do this is to involve the board early on in the process of deciding on the right, big-picture, strategic direction for the company without getting into the details. The CEO and his or her team can develop and present several options to the board, explaining why each has merit. Then the executives can solicit board input on each option but not ask for a vote. In this way, the CEO and his or her team can gain valuable board perspective that will strengthen all the choices that are developed and obtain early buy-in for both the options and the strategic plan that is ultimately chosen.

The CEO can then provide periodic updates on the strategic-planning process through letters to the board and board meetings. This allows the board to stay engaged and provide input but keeps the control over the actual process with the executive team, where it belongs.

Active boards are a corporate reality. How to work with them effectively should be one of the most important items on the CEO agenda. As we have outlined, the CEO has an opportunity not only to manage this new relationship but also to make the active board an asset in building the long-term high performance of the company.

Originally published on hbr.org in August 2017. Reprint H03TTJ

About the Contributors

KEN BANTA is the founder of the Vanguard Forum, a leadership-development program for next-generation CEOs. He is also the principal of the Vanguard Group for Leadership, which advises CEOs and other top executives on leadership and organizational transformation. He was a member of the leadership teams that turned around Pharmacia, Schering-Plough, and Bausch + Lomb.

CLAYTON M. CHRISTENSEN is the Kim B. Clark Professor of Business Administration at Harvard Business School.

CLAUDIO FERNÁNDEZ-ARÁOZ is a senior adviser at the global executive search firm Egon Zehnder and the author of *It's Not the How or the What but the Who* (Harvard Business Review Press, 2014), on which this article is based.

STEPHEN D. GARROW is managing partner at Kayon Partners, a business-development and investment firm, and is entrepreneur-in-residence at the W.R. Berkley Innovation Labs at New York University's Stern School of Business.

DANIEL GOLEMAN, a codirector of the Consortium for Research on Emotional Intelligence in Organizations at Rutgers University, is the author of *Focus: The Hidden Driver of Excellence* (HarperCollins, 2013).

BORIS GROYSBERG is a professor of business administration at Harvard Business School. He is the coauthor (with Michael Slind) of *Talk, Inc: How Trusted Leaders Use Conversations to Power Their Organizations* (Harvard Business Review Press, 2012).

GARY HAMEL is a visiting professor at London Business School and the founder of the Management Lab. He is coauthor of *Humanocracy: Creating Organizations as Amazing as the People Inside Them* (Harvard Business Review Press, forthcoming).

MARK W. JOHNSON is the chairman and a cofounder of Innosight, a strategic innovation and investing company based in Boston.

HENNING KAGERMANN is a former CEO of SAP AG, a software corporation based in Germany.

ROBERT S. KAPLAN is a senior fellow and the Marvin Bower Professor of Leadership Development, Emeritus, at Harvard Business School.

JOHN P. KOTTER is the Konosuke Matsushita Professor of Leadership, Emeritus, at Harvard Business School.

CLAIRE LOVE is a New York—based project leader at BCG's Strategy Institute.

KARLA L. MARTIN was a principal in the San Francisco office of Booz & Company.

ANETTE MIKES is an assistant professor at Harvard Business School.

BANSI NAGJI is a partner at Monitor Group and a leader of the firm's global innovation practice.

GARY L. NEILSON is a Principal with PwC US.

MATTHEW S. OLSON is an executive director at the Corporate Executive Board, an advisory and performance improvement network of leaders of the world's largest public and private organizations, based in Washington, DC. His article is adapted from the book *Stall Points* (Yale University Press, 2008), coauthored with Derek van Bever.

ELIZABETH POWERS was a principal in the New York office of Booz & Company.

C.K. PRAHALAD was the Paul and Ruth McCracken Distinguished Professor of Corporate Strategy at the Stephen M. Ross School of Business at the University of Michigan in Ann Arbor.

MARTIN REEVES is a New York–based senior partner at the Boston Consulting Group and the director of its Strategy Institute.

MICHAEL SLIND is a writer, editor, and communication consultant. He is the coauthor (with Boris Groysberg) of *Talk, Inc: How Trusted Leaders Use Conversations to Power Their Organizations* (Harvard Business Review Press, 2012).

PHILIPP TILLMANNS is a consultant at BCG in Hamburg and a PhD candidate at RWTH Aachen University, in Germany.

GEOFF TUFF is a partner at Monitor Group and a leader of the firm's global innovation practice.

DEREK VAN BEVER is a senior lecturer in the general management unit at Harvard Business School.

SETH VERRY is a senior director at the Corporate Executive Board, an advisory and performance improvement network of leaders of the world's largest public and private organizations, based in Washington, DC.

Index

risk review boards, 194–195
risks, 93
   categories of, 188
   external, 188, 192, 201–205
   identifying, 190–191
   preventable, 188, 190–191
   strategy, 188, 191–192, 194–197

Samsung, 26–27
scenario planning, 203–204. *See also* planning
scorecards, 168–169, 198
searching for loose bricks, 103, 104–105
second-guessing, 157–158
self-awareness, 171–174
self-control, 175–176, 177
70-20-10 balance, 22–25
shadow cabinets, 142
shaping strategy, 3, 8–9
Share at the Marketplace, 85–86
shareholder wealth, 94
share price, 22
Shell Oil, 203
Siemens, 91, 106–107
simulator, organizational-change, 163–169
skills, strategic intent and, 90, 100. *See also* competencies
Slind, Michael, 73–86
smart customization, 160–161
social and emotional learning (SEL), 177
social intelligence, 176–182
social media, 80. *See also* communication; organizational conversation
social sensitivity, 180–182
social thinking, 80–81
Sony, 111
stage-gate processes, 28–29

Stanford University, 174
STC, 91, 106–107
storytelling, 83–84
strategic alliances, 87–88, 91, 96
strategic analysis, 141–142
strategic business units (SBUs), 112–115
strategic fit, 92–93
strategic intent, 87–118
  in brief, 89
  building layers of advantage in, 90–91, 103–104
  changing the terms of engagement and, 103, 105–107
  competing through collaboration and, 103, 106–107
  corporate challenges in, 97–99
  definition of, 90–91
  the essence of winning in, 92–94
  global opportunity/threat analysis and, 111–112
  management and, 91–92
  managing competitive engagements and, 102–103
  misunderstanding rivals', 108–109
  overcommittment to "recipes" and, 112–115
  in practice, 90–92
  reciprocal responsibility and, 101–102
  searching for loose bricks and, 103, 104–105
  stability of, 94
  strategic planning and, 94–96
  strategy hierarchy and, 115–117
  stretch required for, 96–97
  surrender and, 108–110
  target setting in, 94–118
strategic styles
  adaptive, 3, 6–8
  avoiding traps with, 10–13
  in brief, 3

The most important management ideas all in one place.

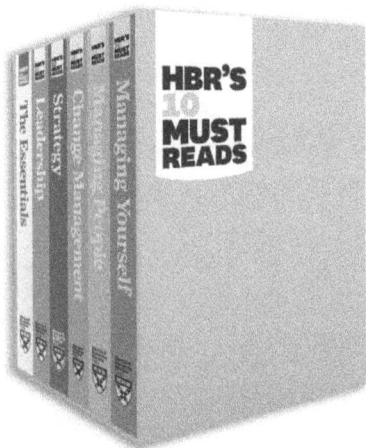

We hope you enjoyed this book from *Harvard Business Review*. Now you can get even more with HBR's 10 Must Reads Boxed Set. From books on leadership and strategy to managing yourself and others, this 6-book collection delivers articles on the most essential business topics to help you succeed.

HBR's 10 Must Reads Series

The definitive collection of ideas and best practices on our most sought-after topics from the best minds in business.

- Change Management
- Collaboration
- Communication
- Emotional Intelligence
- Innovation
- Leadership
- Making Smart Decisions

- Managing Across Cultures
- Managing People
- Managing Yourself
- Strategic Marketing
- Strategy
- Teams
- The Essentials

hbr.org/mustreads

www.ingramcontent.com/pod-product-compliance
Lightning Source LLC
Chambersburg PA
CBHW021118220326
41598CB00052B/1